Get
Writing

Get Writing

A practical guide to creative writing

George Evans · Vince Powell

BBC BOOKS

ISBN 0 563 36027 5

First published 1990

© George Evans and Vince Powell 1990

Published by BBC Books
a division of BBC Enterprises Limited
Woodlands, 80 Wood Lane, London W12 0TT

Set in 10 pt Palatino by Ace Filmsetting Ltd, Frome
Printed and bound in Great Britain by Richard Clay Ltd, Bungay
Cover printed by Richard Clay Ltd, Norwich

Contents

Introduction

In the late nineteenth century in America, they had a rush – the Gold Rush – and here in Britain in the late twentieth century, we, too, have a rush – the Creative Writing Rush.

There is, within us all, the ability to write something. It is true to say that at some time in our lives every one of us has put pen to paper, whether it is to write a letter to a friend, to apply for a job, or merely to send a postcard to Auntie Nellie from Blackpool 'wishing she were there'. The fact that you are at this very moment reading this book is an indication that you are interested in learning a little more about the craft of writing, be it for profit or pleasure.

And if it's profit you prefer, there is no better time than the present. The opportunities for the budding writer are enormous. The number of magazine titles keeps on rising – people have more leisure time and consequently are reading more, and television channels and radio stations are getting more numerous. The market is expanding so rapidly that very soon the demand could well outstrip the supply. You could be part of that supply. You may never achieve such fame as Dennis Potter, Agatha Christie or Alan Ayckbourn, but worry not; there are hundreds of men and women whose names may not be as familiar, but who are nevertheless earning a very good living as writers.

So if you haven't already started writing, now is the time to hitch your wagon to a typewriter, or at the very least, a sheet of paper and a pen. If you have enthusiasm, application, perseverance plus a little bit of talent, then you stand every chance of succeeding.

The public is now becoming more and more aware that writing is not some mystical art confined to professionals. You too can write if you set your mind to it. All you need is to apply yourself to the task diligently. The hardest thing to do is to start. Hopefully, by the time you reach the end of this book you will find it easier to write those first few lines – lines which may eventually lead to your name appearing under the magic words 'written by'. Given the aforementioned enthusiasm and peseverance, coupled with that little bit of luck which we all need, you can do it. But you'll never find out if you don't try. Every successful writer had to begin somewhere. Take us for instance. We were, respectively, a gent's tailor and a cost clerk, but while we were busily costing railway wagons and measuring inside legs, we both had secret ambitions of becoming writers. At the time neither of us ever dreamed that one day we would see our names in print underneath the title of a short story, let alone hear them read out over the air, displayed on a television screen or a theatre bill. But we were both prepared to have a go and try our luck.

They say you need three things to be a writer – dedication, inspiration and perspiration. Well, we had the last in abundance!

Like many would-be writers, we both decided separately to start with the short story. We say separately because at that early stage in our respective careers we hadn't met. It was not until much later when we had both achieved a modicum of success that we began to collaborate.

A short story which George had written was accepted. His joy knew no bounds. The editor telephoned and apologised for the fee, explaining that as he was a new writer, George would be paid the minimum fee. At that moment, George would have paid him!

Around the same time, Vince also had a short story accepted by the now defunct *John Bull* magazine. Like George, he was over the moon. The sales of that magazine increased dramatically that week as Vince bought dozens of copies to send to friends and relations.

After our stories had been published, we both waited expectantly for the telephone to ring – George in his little cottage in Wales, and Vince in his semi in Manchester. Surely it was only a question of time before the editor of *Punch*, or somebody at the BBC or ITV read our stories, recognised our talents and made us an offer we couldn't refuse. Alas, the telephone remained silent, and we slowly realised that we still had a mountain to climb. Doggedly we struggled on; eventually, many rejection slips later, we succeeded, and both jointly and separately went on to write many scripts for radio, television, stage and cinema.

Can *you* do it, too? Of course you can – but only if you try. You won't know if you don't try! Many wiseacres say 'Oh, nobody can teach people to write. The only way to write and improve is to write and write.' Certainly you can write and write, but if you start off on the wrong foot you continue on the wrong foot. Our aim is to point you in the right direction from the start, and to show you how to use your ideas, imagination and talent to their best advantage.

Interested? Then read on . . .

GEORGE EVANS and VINCE POWELL

May 1990

1. How To Get Started

What motivates people to become writers? In a majority of cases, it is the urge for self-expression – to communicate one's thoughts, ideas and beliefs to others. And in some cases, it is sheer exasperation.

How many times, we wonder, has the following conversation taken place?

HIM   Did you watch that new sitcom last night on the telly?
HER   No. Was it any good?
HIM   It didn't make me laugh once.
HER   What was it about?
HIM   It was about half an hour too long! I could write better stuff with my eyes shut.
HER   So could I.

Perhaps you too have had this conversation at some time or another. If so, what have you done about it? If you really think that you can write better, then go ahead and do it. Pick up a pen, get a notebook and start jotting down ideas. Instead of staring out of the window of the bus or train on your way to work, use the time constructively to think of ideas, plots and characters. You'll soon get caught in the 'writer's web' – your enthusiasm will grow until you can hardly wait to get cracking and start writing. You'll be hooked. Writing is like that.

'Ah,' you may ask, 'but how can I be a writer? I don't know enough about it!' Well, there are several ways to learn about the techniques of creative writing. Many further education centres now have courses in creative writing, so why not see if yours does, and if so go along and join the class. Don't worry – it won't be full of intellectuals discussing the meaning of Dostoyevsky's *The Brothers Karamazov*. Your class will be far more likely to consist of people of various ages from all walks of life – students, senior citizens, typists, housewives, sales executives, shop assistants, maybe the odd yuppy or two. All your classmates have a common bond and objective, that of wanting to translate their thoughts, ideas and experiences into the written word.

Remember whichever medium you choose to write for, be it radio, television, books, theatre, films or poetry, certain forms of writing require particular techniques, and these will be discussed and explained later on in the book. But for the moment, let us commence with some of the basic principles.

Tools of the trade

Firstly, what do you need? Well, apart from pen and paper, there are a few other essentials which every prospective writer should have.

To start with you will need a dictionary. Nobody likes to read a badly spelt manuscript, so please use a dictionary. There are many from which to choose – we use the *Concise Oxford Dictionary*, but there are other equally good ones on the market.

Another extremely useful book for any writer is a thesaurus, of which the most popular appears to be *Roget's Thesaurus*. What is the difference, you may ask, between a dictionary and a thesaurus? Well, a dictionary confines itself to giving you the precise meaning of a word, whereas a thesaurus will give you several alternatives to a word, which helps you not to be repetitive. For example, suppose you want another word meaning cheap, which you have already used. Look in a thesaurus and you will find it lists twenty-three alternatives, including inexpensive, moderate, economical, low-priced, two a penny, reasonable and so on. So you see, a thesaurus is invaluable.

We would also recommend you get a copy of the *Oxford Dictionary of Quotations*. Not only is it useful for finding suitable quotes to add colour to your dialogue, it is a wonderful source of titles. Just consider how many quotations have provided titles for literary works. *The Paths of Glory* was taken from Thomas Gray's 'Elegy written in a Country Churchyard'; *Till Death Us Do Part* came from the *Book of Common Prayer*. *Fools Rush In*, the title of a successful play, then a film, and much later, of a popular song, came from Alexander Pope's 'An Essay on Criticism'.

These three books are the tools of your trade. There are others you may wish to acquire, such as Harrap's *English Usage* or a dictionary of synonyms, but the three we have suggested are a must. They will help you to use words in the most effective way and they also contribute to make writing more enjoyable and interesting.

We have earlier referred to pen and paper, but these are to be used purely for jotting down notes or scribbling down a rough draft. Your final draft, when ready for submission, should always be typewritten.

We realise that typewriters are expensive, but it is possible to pick up a second-hand machine fairly cheaply. Failing that, you may be able to borrow a typewriter from a friend. If you can afford it you could use a secretarial agency.

Again, for those of you who can afford it, there are many comparatively cheap word processors on the market these days and they are well worth the investment. Whatever you do, we stress the importance of submitting clear, typewritten manuscripts. Many editors will not even read hand-written submissions.

Studying the market

It is vitally important that you study your particular market thoroughly, in order to send your manuscript to the right place. If you have written a romantic love story, it doesn't make much sense to submit it to *Private Eye* or *Mechanics' Weekly* unless you're collecting rejection slips. You may think we're being facetious, but it has been known. Before you even begin to find ways of expressing your ideas you should make a thorough study of the particular market you are aiming at; this applies equally to radio, television, magazines or book publishing. If you do this, you will know exactly for whom you are writing and what they are looking for.

Let us assume for instance, that you have an idea for a short story, which you hope to submit to a particular women's magazine. Buy that magazine and read it from cover to cover. Read the editorial, the agony column, the readers' letters, the articles and, of course, the short stories. By doing this you will discover what kind of readership the magazine is aimed at. It is essential that you know this. If your romantic love story is about a middle-aged affair, the editor of a magazine aimed at teenagers is hardly likely to welcome it with open arms, let alone an open cheque-book. It might be the best love story ever written, but if it doesn't land on the right desk you might just as well not have written it.

The same applies equally to radio and television. Watch, listen and digest the programme content before you submit anything. A radio situation comedy won't get any smiles from the producer of *Woman's Hour*; similarly, the BBC's Head of Light Entertainment is not in the market for a half-hour drama.

So we repeat, do your market research thoroughly in the beginning and you'll find that it will pay dividends in the end. It's time and effort well spent.

Before we move on to the next stage of the book in which we show you how to find ideas by using our 'idea awareness' method, let us summarise the points we have made so far.

1 Identify the urge to write.
2 Equip yourself with the tools of the trade.
3 Believe in yourself. You can do it if you try.
4 Don't waste your spare time. Make it work for you.
5 Research your market thoroughly at the beginning. If you don't, you will find that you're writing in a vacuum.

What you have read up to now seems to be mainly concerned with writing for profit, but the same basic rules apply equally to writing for pleasure, with which we will deal in a later chapter. Suffice to say that a letter to a newspaper or an article in your church magazine deserve just as much care, application and thought as does a short story to be sent to an editor.

So far, so good. It's been relatively easy up to now, hasn't it? It's time to start getting down to the nitty-gritty.

2. *Idea Awareness*

It's all in the mind

Ideas are the life blood of every writer – whatever you choose to write, the idea has to come first, and most important, it has to be the right idea. You will find that with the right idea, the actual writing itself will come much more easily, whereas the wrong idea will cause you many long hours of hard, unfruitful labour as you struggle to turn it into a short story or play. Inevitably you will end up by rejecting it and having to start looking for another idea, something which you should have done when you began to experience difficulty in developing the first one. Many writers, having had an idea which they initially thought promising, are unwilling to part with it. They spend days desperately trying to make it work rather than throwing it away. Don't fall into this trap. At the first inkling of trouble, be brave. Reject it and go back to the drawing board. You will save yourself an awful lot of time and trouble.

Whether your ultimate ambition is to write a short story, an article, a radio play or a television drama, it's the idea that counts, and in broad terms, there is virtually no difference in your approach to finding the right idea for whatever project you have in mind – the only difference is in how you develop your idea and tailor it to your chosen subject.

Each medium, whether it be radio, television, theatre, magazines or books, has certain technical requirements of the writer. We shall be exploring these in much greater depth in subsequent chapters, but before continuing with the theme of idea awareness, it will be useful for you to be aware of the various needs of each medium.

The printed word

Articles
The market for articles is enormous. Every newspaper, every

trade journal, every magazine is constantly on the look-out for entertaining and informative articles of anything between 750 and 2000 words. Naturally, most trade journals are interested only in articles concerning their particular trade or industry but an article doesn't always have to be a technical one. If you drive a car, you may well have a real life experience to write about. A humorous account of a breakdown; what you did while waiting for the AA to arrive; how to keep children entertained during a long car journey. A motoring magazine may well be interested in a light-hearted article as a change from its more technical ones. You've most certainly dined out somewhere during your lifetime. Did you have an interesting or amusing experience in a restaurant or hotel? If so, then a catering magazine may be happy to publish it. Was your holiday last year a disaster? Your account of it may interest a travel magazine. Do you have a particular hobby? If so, you may well be able to write an article about it.

Short stories for magazines
As with articles, the short story market is vast. The length of your story can vary depending upon the way you develop your idea. It can be as little as 1000 words or as much as 8–9000 words. The subject matter can be whatever you wish to write about – a love story, a mystery, or whatever, but, as we mentioned earlier, first decide what you want to write about and tailor your ideas accordingly. And don't forget to submit your story to the appropriate publication.

Short stories for radio
BBC Radio 4 are constantly on the look-out for contributors to their *Morning Story* slot and also occasionally for stories to include in *Woman's Hour*, and producers are very keen to encourage new writers who are trying to establish themselves. The running time of a short story on radio is usually 15 minutes, which is roughly about 2000 words. When searching for a suitable idea you should bear in mind that your story will be read on the air by a professional actor or actress, who will heighten the interest for the listener by assuming the various voices of the characters in your story. As there are only so many different voices that a narrator can reasonably be expected to have in his or her repertoire, it would not be practical to fill your story with a cast of thousands. Too many characters tend to confuse the listener and we would advise you to confine yourself to three or four characters.

As far as the subject matter is concerned, you should bear in mind that *Morning Story* is broadcast at 10.30 a.m., so that a producer will not look too kindly on stories of a *risqué* nature. The use of bad language is also frowned upon. You may be tempted to think that the odd swear word or two helps to make a point in your story, but in nearly every case they only turn out to be an embarrassment.

When you are searching for a short story idea for radio, as opposed to a play idea, beware of dream sequences and 'true' stories of war-time experiences. There have been so many of these in the past that yet more along these lines are unlikely to be considered at present. The most important ingredient looked for, and this applies to all forms of creative writing, is originality, both in the idea and its subsequent development.

Short stories for television
It may come as a surprise to you but short stories are often read on television. Every television channel, whether BBC or ITV, produces programmes aimed specifically at the younger viewers – programmes such as *Rainbow*, *Blue Peter*, *Jackanory* and so on, in which, from time to time, short stories are read by well-known personalities. These stories are from five to ten minutes in duration and may occasionally take the form of a serial if they are much longer. A five minute story would consist of approximately 700 words, and whilst many producers commission established children's writers or use already published material, some are quite willing to consider submissions from new writers.

As writing for children is a highly specialised area, it is more important than ever that you study the market very carefully before you put pen to paper. You should make every effort to keep your idea simple. However, this does not mean that you should write down to your audience. Children today are quite perceptive at an early age. Providing that your subject matter is appealing to young children, and that you avoid words like 'disestablishmentarianism' you don't have to write using words of one syllable.

Drama for radio
If writing a play is what you wish to do, then the radio play is perhaps the best starting point for a new writer. Many of today's leading playwrights began by writing for radio. For the enthusiastic wordsmith, radio is arguably the most satisfying medium for

drama. If you have a love for words, radio provides you with the opportunity to use them to the fullest advantage. The radio play gives the writer very wide opportunities for using ideas, situations and dialogue to stimulate the listener's imagination. If the right inflection is used the spoken word can convey far greater depth and meaning than the written word alone. Another great plus for radio is that the writer is not bound by the limitations of television drama, films or the stage play. Radio has none of the restrictions caused by being tied to a certain number of studio sets; there are no problems with costly outside film sequences which you will encounter in writing for television. The theatre, too, has its limitations in terms of the stage set and the cast. Most theatrical producers tend to prefer a play to take place in one set and with as few characters as possible.

The radio play, however, gives the writer total freedom. You can set your play anywhere you care to. In the twinkling of an eye, you can transport the listener from London to Venice, with a scene on the Orient Express in between. You can write a play set in Moscow's Red Square, or on an ocean liner, if you want to.

The BBC Radio Drama Department is always more than willing to read original plays by new writers. The length of a radio play can vary from half an hour (about 4500 words) to one and a half hours (about 13 000 words). As in the case of short stories, plays with a contemporary theme are far more likely to get accepted than historical plays or plays set in the future. However, there are always exceptions to every rule, and if you have written a stunning play with sparkling dialogue set in outer space, it just *could* be accepted. But our advice at this early stage in your writing career is to keep it contemporary.

As far as the subject matter for a radio play is concerned, the world is your oyster. It could be a thriller, a love story, a tragedy or a comedy – what it must never be is too predictable.

Drama for television
Writing for televison has its own particular set of rules and requirements which will be discussed in Chapter 6, but as you try and find a suitable idea on which to base your play, the one thing you must keep uppermost in your mind is that your idea should be capable of development in visual terms. Long scenes of dialogue between two characters without anything visual taking place can be extremely tedious and are calculated to have the viewer changing channels rapidly.

So remember that although interesting dialogue is always necessary for whichever medium you are writing, where television is concerned you must constantly aim for visual ideas and images. Plays on television can be as short as half an hour (about 3500 words) and as long as two hours (about 14 000 words). You will notice that the number of words required for a television play is less than for a radio play; this is to allow for its visual content. If, when you have written it, your play has more words than we have quoted, then it isn't visual enough. Today the television play can cover a very wide range of subjects, some of which, like infidelity or homosexuality, were previously taboo, but if you treat such subjects sensitively, you are far more likely to get your play accepted than if it is designed to shock.

Stage plays

A stage play is normally about two hours in length – about 14 000 words, depending on the amount of visual activity within the play.

Possibly the first important thing to think about here is cost, because this can be the reason why a play, no matter how good it is, doesn't see the light of day. This applies to both amateur and professional productions. Consider the cost of the set, the scenery, and the costumes, and keep all to the minimum. It could make that vital difference.

Generally speaking, when you develop an idea for a stage play, it is a good policy to construct it so that all the action takes place inside one set. In fact, many contemporary plays don't have a conventional set at all. Lighting and props are used to create 'place' and occasion, sometimes very effectively.

So think of the practicalities first; if you make your play an economic possibility you're off to a good start.

This section should have given you an idea of what you're up against initially. So we'll return to the theme of finding ideas, and how to go about this.

Finding the right idea

One of the most difficult problems facing the new writer is finding a suitable idea which can be developed into an entertaining story or play. Some new writers sit for hours staring at a blank sheet of paper, waiting for inspiration to strike. Don't make that mistake. The only thing likely to strike you is cramp!

Ideas are, in fact, not all that difficult to find. All you need to know is where and how to look for them. We call this 'idea awareness'. The simple truth is that there are ideas all around you. Think about it. You only have to pick up a newspaper and read it carefully with 'awareness'. You will discover at least half a dozen ideas which could spark off a story or a play. As we are writing this chapter, we have just picked up a copy of today's newspaper and looked through it. Here are just a couple of news items that, with 'idea awareness', could be successfully developed into either a short story or a play for radio or television.

IRATE WIFE LOCKS HUSBAND OUT OF HOUSE

A Mr James Hudson, retired builder from Gwent, returned home from his local last night, only to find that his wife Ruth had locked him out of the house. After shouting abuse, Mr Hudson threw a dustbin through the front room window, and in trying to climb through, cut himself severely. He was taken to hospital where he had eighteen stitches put in his leg. Both he and his wife have refused to make any statement to the police, who have said that no charges will be preferred as it is a domestic matter.

Read that report carefully and consider the many different options it presents you as a writer.

Why did Ruth lock her husband out of the house?

Was she simply fed up of being left on her own night after night, while her husband was drinking with his cronies?

Or was it his cronies he was drinking with?

Perhaps he was having an affair and Ruth had found out.

Or was Ruth a shrewish woman. Did her husband go out to escape her nagging?

Did he come back from the pub particularly early that night, and find the door locked because Ruth was entertaining a gentleman friend?

The more you think about it, the more opportunities for development you will find it gives you.

Another item which caught our eye was a photograph of a young woman, underneath which was the caption 'Do you know this woman?' The item went on to reveal that the woman had been discovered by police wandering along the hard shoulder of the M1, near the Newport Pagnell service station. When questioned she couldn't tell them who she was or where she came from. The only clue to her identity was a return bus ticket from Sheffield found in her handbag, which was otherwise empty. To apply our 'idea awareness' method, ask yourself these questions:

How? Why? When? Who?

How did she get on the M1. How did she lose her memory? She may be feigning.

Why was her handbag empty? Had she been robbed?

When did she get off the bus? And for what reason? Was she running away from somebody?

Who is she? Who was she going to see? Has she been reported missing?

All these questions can help you start to develop this item into a play or story. And every day in every paper you will find items which, given an inventive mind, can provide you with lots of ideas.

But 'idea awareness' isn't just about reading items in the newspapers. It's based on observation, and training yourself to look for ideas in everyday life. When you are travelling to and from work in the bus or train, look at your travelling companions sitting around you. Study their faces, their mannerisms, their clothing. Ask yourself where they are going, what they do, what's in his briefcase or her handbag. Scribble down a description of them, and try to invent a situation in which they could be involved.

Is the man involved in industrial espionage? Perhaps his briefcase contains the designs for a revolutionary engine which he plans to sell to a rival company. Is the girl with a shopping bag on her way to the first day of a new job? Has she a boyfriend? Is she married with a lover?

The day is full of opportunities for you to find ideas. It's all a question of keeping your eyes open wherever you go. In the supermarket; in the pub; at the shops; at a football match. Every little incident could provide you with an idea. That abandoned car for instance. Is there a story that you could weave around it? Why has it been abandoned? Has it been stolen? Who does it belong to? How many owners has it previously had? This is what 'idea awareness' is all about – to look on every object and incident as a potential source of material. It really works – believe us. It worked for Terence Rattigan. He took an idea about the various owners of a car and wrote it as a screenplay. It was called *The Yellow Rolls Royce*. When the late Georges Simenon wanted a theme for a new novel he spent three months walking round Paris with a notebook observing people and places, jotting down snatches of conversation and trivial incidents as he looked for a suitable idea.

You should do the same. Always have a notebook and pencil handy, and your mind alert to any possibilities. You may pass an empty shop. Quite an ordinary everyday sight. Nothing there for an idea, you may think. But stop and think about what lies behind the 'For Sale' sign? Was there a time, perhaps, when a proud new owner, full of enthusiasm and ambition, dreamt of building an empire from that one shop? What happened? Did the business fail? Was there a domestic problem? Was there perhaps a supernatural reason that drove him out?

Similarly you may be walking along a street full of ordinary looking semi-detached houses. Look at each house as you pass. Try to imagine what sort of people live behind those doors. Each house has a different story to tell. Tales of drama, happiness, tragedy and love. Using 'idea awareness' you can invent stories round all these subjects. *Coronation Street* has been doing it for over thirty years. So could you.

Another useful source for obtaining ideas is from your own life. Nobody leads a totally bland and uneventful life – not even you. Go back over your life. Try to recall any incidents from the past. Your first day at school, if you can remember that far back! Holidays with the family; your first job; that first teenage love affair; a death in the family. Sit down with your notebook and jot down as many things from your early life as you can recall. At least one of them should provide you with a good idea.

Look at James Herriot, the famous veterinary surgeon, and all those wonderfully entertaining stories he wrote based on autobiographical incidents, which eventually became a successful television series. Read the short stories of Ernest Hemingway, Somerset Maugham and Paul Gallico. Many of them are based on true incidents in which they were personally involved. Some of those stories have been made into television plays and films.

So we repeat. Observe, inquire and note. Ask your friends about themselves. Try to find out what experiences, humorous or dramatic, have happened to them. You'll find that they'll be only too pleased to tell you. Most people love talking about themselves. Strike up a conversation with a stranger. You could run the risk of being cold-shouldered, but on the other hand you could find another idea, and perhaps a new friend in the process. You will find ideas come to you more easily as you continue to develop 'idea awareness'. After a while you will automatically begin to see possibilities in all sorts of incidents, on which you can build your story, play or film. The more you read, the more you observe, the more you discover, the more receptive your mind will become.

And, of course, it goes without saying that whatever it is that you have decided to write, you must find out as much about it as you possibly can. If it's a short story that you feel you want to write, read as many as you can lay your hands on. Try to discover the basic ideas behind each story. You'll find in many cases that the story springs from a very simple idea. If you prefer the idea of writing a play, listen to *Saturday Night Theatre* on Radio 4, watch plays on television and go to the theatre as often as you can. Note how the writer uses visual action to enhance the entertainment value of his of her television or stage play. Similarly consider how valuable sound effects can be in a radio play – a creaking door, an owl hooting, the wind whistling through the trees can create a sense of foreboding. It is so very important to get to know as much as you can about the particular medium on which you have decided to concentrate.

It's a strange thing, but writing is perhaps the only profession for which there is no recognised professional course of study. There is no apprenticeship period of training, no examination to pass, no diploma to have on your wall. Some people send a script in, it's accepted and bingo! Overnight a writer is born. This happened to a writer called Raymond Allen. He was an unknown, living on the Isle of Wight, and he wrote a half-hour comedy script which he sent to the BBC. It landed on the desk of the late Michael Mills, who at the time was Head of Comedy. Michael read the script, liked it and sent it to another Michael – Michael Crawford, who also read it and liked it. The result was *Some Mothers Do 'Ave 'Em*, one of the BBC's most successful situation comedy series. On the debit side, however, there are many people who spend years sending in ideas and scripts before having anything accepted. Luck as well as talent plays a great part in the risky business of writing.

In 1903, Somerset Maugham, then aged 29, wrote a play called *Lady Frederick* and by 1907 it had been turned down by no less than 17 managements. He was discouraged and disillusioned; he decided that he was a failure as a writer. Some years previously, he had trained as a physician and surgeon at St Thomas' Hospital in London and he made up his mind to return to the hospital, take a refresher course, and apply for a course as a ship's surgeon. Luck, however, was about to play its part. The manager of the Royal Court Theatre had a surprise failure. A play which had been booked for a two month run suddenly proved a disaster and was taken off, leaving the Royal Court with a gap of six weeks, and nothing to fill it. Maugham promptly sent his play to the manager, who, more out of desperation than anything else, agreed to put it on. *Lady Frederick*, the play that had been rejected 17 times, opened at the Royal Court on 26 October 1907 and ran for 422 performances, launching Maugham on an uninterrupted writing career that was to last for a lifetime (and depriving the Royal Navy of a surgeon).

The lesson to be learned from these examples is never to give up. If you believe in what you have written, someday, somebody else will believe in it too. You are likely to experience many setbacks along the rocky road which leads to success – indeed you may feel as if you will never reach the end of the road, but don't be discouraged. The important thing is to get on that road. As Robert Louis Stevenson put it 'To travel hopefully is a better thing than to arrive, and the true success is to labour.' So pick up that pen, open that notebook and go out in search of an idea.

Using our 'idea awareness' technique will enable you to discover lots of ideas for your particular project. But remember our earlier advice. Before you start to write your idea, make absolutely certain that it is the right one, and capable of being developed.

Finally, before we move on to explain how to develop your idea, a word of warning. Whatever idea you happen to think of must have a strong situation, preferably one with which the listener or viewer can identify and, most important, it must be about relationships and attitudes. Many ideas which at first glance seem perfectly viable often end in failure purely because they were not based on relationships. Here is an example. Some years ago, Thames Television were looking for an idea for a series suitable for the late Sid James. A couple of writers who shall be nameless, but not blameless, suggested a comedy series set in a betting shop, with Sid as the manager. It seemed on the surface a reasonable idea and a pilot script was commissioned. When it arrived it seemed a funny enough script, in which Sid was involved in a scheme to fiddle a betting slip so that he won a small fortune. The writers were then asked to supply some brief story lines for further episodes. They thought of one other plot, then ran out of ideas.

And when you think about it, it wasn't surprising. There aren't many stories which can be done in a betting shop except for stories about betting, and that can become very limiting. All good sitcoms have strong character relationships to hold them together, not just an amusing background. There were no strong relationships in the pilot script. Sid was single – he had no real connection with anyone other than his dim-witted assistant. So the idea was rejected. Not so long after, two other writers came up with the idea of putting Sid into a domestic situation, with a wife, a daughter and a layabout son. It was called *Bless This House* and ran for several years.

Look at *Steptoe and Son*. You may think it was about two rag and bone men, but it wasn't only that. It was about a love–hate relationship between a father and his son. Neither could do without the other no matter how they tried. The fact that they were rag and bone men added to the situation, but it was only incidental. *Steptoe* would have been just as successful had they been dustmen or run a transport café. Relationships mean emotions – love, hatred, passion and conflict – and whatever you write the characters you create should strike a chord of recognition in the viewer, the listener or the reader.

Summing up

So, just to summarise before we move on to 'idea development':

1 Be observant. Keep your eyes and ears open at all times.
2 Try to be original.
3 Read magazines, listen to the radio, watch television, and go to the theatre.
4 Make sure your idea can be developed.
5 Remember the importance of everyday reality and relationships.
6 Don't be easily discouraged. Keep trying and it will happen.

3. Idea Development and the Short Story

Start at the end

Starting at the end isn't, as you may think, a contradiction in terms. We'll explain. Before you sit down to start fleshing out and developing your idea into a plot or synopsis you must first give some thought as to how that idea is going to turn out. You need to have a clear sense of direction – a finish to work toward. It's rather like a builder who sets out to build a house; before he starts to dig the foundations, he must have an architect's plan to work from. He has to know what the finished building will look like. He can't start halfway through, then suddenly decide to add an extra room upstairs or tack on a conservatory. He has to work to a plan.

Similarly, before you start to develop your idea, you must have your own plan, so that you know exactly where and how you are going to finish your short story or play. All forms of writing, articles, short stories, plays or books, follow three basic rules. They must have a beginning, a middle and an end. The beginning is usually where your characters and theme are introduced. Then you should direct your thoughts towards creating a dramatic or humorous climax, which will leave your reader, listener or viewer with a feeling of satisfaction. If your ending is inconclusive, and leaves too many loose ends unresolved, the audience will be left with a feeling of disappointment – of somehow being cheated. Of course, rules are sometimes made to be broken, and occasionally a writer will end his story or play without any definite conclusion, leaving a challenge to the imagination – will the husband ever be reconciled with his wife, or did the butler *really* do it? As far as a new and inexperienced writer is concerned, however, we recommend that you work to a more conventional conclusion.

We should make it clear, at this point, that we are referring to short stories, plays and novels, and not serials like *EastEnders* or *Coronation Street*, or stories serialised in women's magazines, in which each episode has to end unresolved, in order to tempt the reader/viewer to read or watch the following episode.

So how do you think of a suitable ending for your idea? As you progress, you will discover that many of your ideas will quite often provide you with an obvious ending. For example, let us assume you have an idea for a murder mystery. It should be obvious to you that as you develop your idea it is absolutely necessary to determine how the mystery ends and who is the guilty party before you can even begin to start thinking of working out the middle.

Or perhaps you have an idea for a romantic love story. In order to develop the plot more fully you will first have to decide in your own mind how the story will end. Will it be a conventional 'happy-ever-after' ending or will it end in tears and tragedy? Then, and only then, can you really start to flesh out the bare bones of your idea.

The middle

Having got your beginning and your end sorted out, you are now in a position to concentrate on the most important part – the middle, which is where you will need all your ingenuity, skill and inventiveness to hold the audience's interest. Indeed, if you fail to do this, they may never get to the end. You might have the best, most exciting beginning ever written, but if you don't follow that with a gripping and entertaining middle, you will have lost your people long before the end. The middle should be so good that the reader can't put the book down, the listener turn off the radio or the viewer switch over to another channel.

A good middle should contain at least some, if not all, of the following ingredients: conflict; suspense; pathos; humour; and drama.

It is probably true to say that the two most popular themes for short stories or plays are romance and crime. So let us look at these two themes by turn and examine how we could take an idea and develop it so that there is a beginning, a middle and an end. First, let's take romance, where you could be writing either a short story or a play for radio or television. Romance generally implies that two people are in love, so your beginning should introduce your two main characters – let's call them Jack and Jill. Now let's try and find a good ending. It could have a happy ending, and there's nothing wrong with that as long as there's enough drama and excitement along the way, but for the object of this little exercise let's try and find a more unconventional ending.

Does it end in a tragedy – a death, perhaps? That's fairly unconventional. Right, we'll settle for that. How about the middle? Jack meets Jill. How did they meet? Was it on a blind date? Or was she waiting to park her car and he pinched her parking space? Perhaps they met at a dance, in a supermarket, in the post office. Think of somewhere interesting and unusual where they could have met. Make a list: a bank; a cinema; a hospital; a garage; a library; a church – a church! That's unusual. They met in a church. Was Jack a priest and Jill a nun? No, that's a little too unconventional. But a church is good – a Roman Catholic church, say. Why were they there? What were they doing? Were they both attending Mass? That would imply that they were both Catholics, so where's the conflict? If one of them *isn't* a Catholic, what are they doing in a Catholic church? Perhaps the conflict comes from one of them being married. Could be, but it's been done before. Is there anything more original? Perhaps Jack ought to be a Protestant and they meet somewhere else. Religious bigotry has always been a good source of conflict. Look at Northern Ireland. Wait a minute – now there's a good idea. Do we set it in Northern Ireland and make Jack a British soldier? That's better. There's even more scope for conflict. Jill's family would hate him for being Protestant and British. Now, where and how did they meet? Pity about the church – that seemed such a good idea, but what reason can we think of for a Protestant British soldier to be in a Catholic church in Northern Ireland? Can you think of one? Well, let's go back a little. Jack doesn't need to be a Protestant. We've got enough conflict with him being a British soldier. So he *could* be a Catholic, and they could meet when they both attend Mass. This will immediately give us much more scope for the subsequent development. Jack could find himself in a very difficult situation, especially if Jill's family espouse the Republican cause. He might be torn between loyalty to his country and his love for Jill.

So, remembering that we are working toward a tragic end, there are a couple of options open to us. Because of the opposition from her parents, Jill decides to leave home. She arranges to meet Jack at his army camp, but as she arrives a bomb attack takes place and she is killed, ironically by her own side. Maybe one of her brothers is a member of the group of bombers. Or, equally ironic, perhaps Jack wins her parents over, they go out to a predominantly Catholic pub to celebrate and Jack falls victim to a Unionist attack.

We have, literally, been making all this up as we went along to demonstrate our technique for 'idea development'. There are lots of other ways you could develop the idea further; at their first meeting Jack could be wearing civilian clothes so that it would come as a shock when we discover that he is a British soldier. Jill could be ordered by her father to end her association with Jack. Jack could discover that Jill's brother is an active member of the IRA. We're sure you can all see the many possibilities which an idea like this can provide you with, and we hope that we have illustrated how to use your thought processes to build your idea into a synopsis or outline. From here you can start to write your story or play. Of course, when you actually get down to the writing you will need even more inventiveness, but we will deal with that in a later chapter.

We've looked at the romantic theme, so now let's turn our attention to crime. The main points of any crime storyline are:

1 A crime is committed, usually a robbery or a murder (the beginning).
2 An investigation is mounted (the middle).
3 The thief or murderer is revealed (the end).

When you start to develop this kind of idea, it is most important to grab peoples' attention from the word go. The crime should be imaginative and bold – for example, a plot to burgle the Royal Mint or a body found in a room, in which the door and windows are locked from the inside, and there is no apparent way that a murderer could have entered. So be inventive, be daring, think big. We already know that the only satisfactory conclusion is the solving of the crime and the unmasking of the perpetrator, so the middle must contain the method – how the crime was committed – and the motive. When developing the middle of a crime or murder mystery, your first duty to the audience is to mystify, baffle and perplex; to devise so many red herrings and so many false trails that nobody can possible guess who the guilty party is until you reveal it. Every character should have a motive – a reason to have committed the crime. Nobody should have a clear-cut alibi, so that they are all suspects. Let us give you an example of one way that a 'murder in a locked room' mystery could be developed.

1 **The beginning:** a police inspector arrives at the country house of Sir John Barker. He is admitted by Sir John's son,

David. There are four other people present, who have been invited to dinner by Sir John. The Inspector reveals that ten minutes previously, Sir John had telephoned the police station to say that he had reason to suspect that one of his dinner guests was planning to murder him. David tells the Inspector that some twenty minutes ago, his father excused himself and went into his study saying he had some important business to attend to. When David leads the Inspector to the study, they find the door locked and bolted from the inside. There is no response to their knocking. They go outside to the french windows, which are also locked and bolted from the inside. Through a gap in the curtains, the Inspector sees Sir John slumped, unmoving, over his desk. David smashes the window and rushes to his father. He raises him up and gasps in horror. The Inspector quickly moves across and David points to a stiletto piercing his father's heart.

2 **The middle:** the Inspector questions the dinner guests. They are David, Tony Wilson (Sir John's business partner) and his wife Marcia, Miriam Hopkins (Sir John's personal secretary) and Charles Watkins (Sir John's accountant).

He discovers that Sir John welcomed his guests, then, after David had poured everyone a drink, Sir John went into his study taking his drink with him. From that moment until the time the body was discovered, nobody had left the lounge. During his investigation, the Inspector finds that each guest had a motive for killing Sir John: David had huge gambling debts which could now be settled as he is the sole beneficiary of his father's estate; Tony, the business partner had discovered that Sir John had been his wife's lover for the past couple of years, and Marcia had just been dropped by Sir John in favour of a younger mistress; Miriam hated her employer because he had sacked her father, who had become so depressed at not being able to get another job that he had committed suicide; and Sir John had just found out that Charles had been fiddling the company accounts, and was about to expose him.

We are faced with an insoluble crime. Although motives were there in abundance, method and opportunity were absent. How could Sir John have been killed in a room that was locked and bolted from the inside? And who did it? None of the guests left the lounge from the time Sir John was last seen alive on his way to the study to the time he was found dead. It would appear to be impossible. But the Inspector remembers the words which Sir Arthur Conan Doyle had put into the mouth of his most famous creation, Sherlock Holmes: 'When you have eliminated the impossible, whatever remains, however improbable, must be the truth!'

3 **The end:** the Inspector returns to the study. He picks up the almost empty brandy balloon from which Sir John had been drinking and puts a drop on his tongue. He calls all the guests in and reveals that he knows who the murderer is and how it was done. It was David. When he poured his father a drink, he slipped in a drug which he knew would render him unconscious in 15 minutes. It was he, pretending to be his father, who telephoned the police, and it was he who was the first person to reach his father, after smashing the french window. As the Inspector was climbing through, David swiftly stabbed his father with a stiletto which he had previously concealed.

We have deliberately included in this development of the crime idea all the elements needed for the success of a short story, play or novel. Read it again carefully. The crime itself and particularly the method was out of the ordinary, and very carefully worked out. All the characters appear to have a motive and most important, the developed idea presents the audience with a challenge. The appeal of a crime for most people lies in the challenge to solve it before the writer reveals the solution. However, in order to present the challenge, the writer must be fair and give all the relevant facts and clues. Nothing must be hidden. In the example we have given, all the information is there for the people to attempt to work it out. One very famous crime writer, Ellery Queen, often used to have a paragraph before the final dénouement, headed 'Challenge to the Reader' in which he summed up the crime and invited the reader to try and arrive at the right solution before reading on.

We hope that you will find these practical illustrations of ways of developing ideas useful to you. At the outset of this chapter we said that the basic rules of 'idea development' can be applied to all forms of writing, but certain rules apply to particular forms of writing, and you should be aware of these.

Articles

The main point to keep in mind about writing an article is that articles are about facts, not fiction, although it is sometimes permissible to dress up your article with a little light fiction. A straightforward account of an event can sometimes make very boring reading. A little artistic licence can brighten up the dullest article. The secret of article writing is first to know your subject thoroughly and even more important, to make it interesting. Naturally, all writing must be interesting enough to make your reader want to carry on, but with fiction it is easier to do this as you have a much broader canvas to work on. An article, being based on facts, is much more difficult. You must try to present your material or technical information as attractively as possible. Make it entertaining to read as well as educational and informative. If you do that then whatever facts and figures you are trying to impart will be more easily absorbed and remembered by your reader. We have already discussed how to find ideas for writing an article. Developing an idea is simply a question of expanding it. Check your facts – make sure you've got them right. Search for a better turn of phrase, a clever *bon mot* or an apt and amusing quotation to help make your article more appealing. Perhaps we can best illustrate this by giving you an example. The following article is an object lesson on getting the best out of an ordinary subject.

GETTING THERE CAN BE FUN TOO

It was five o'clock in the morning on July 31st. Dawn was breaking, and I was about to do something that I do at the same time and on the same day every year – load our estate car for our annual summer holiday in the south of France.

Naturally, it was raining!

We have been taking the car to France for several years now, partly because I prefer to have our own familiar vehicle, and partly because, with VAT in France at 33⅓%, hiring a car over there is very expensive. Also, with two young children it's very useful to be able to take their favourite toys, buckets and spades – and we usually take along a couple of airbeds, four canvas beach chairs, an inflatable boat, a cool box, two beach umbrellas, travelling iron, heated rollers, a hair dryer and twice as many clothes as we need!

About an hour later, after the car had been loaded, unloaded and reloaded again, which also happens every year, it was time to set off. Getting to Dover these days is simple from practically any part of the country. It's nearly all motorway. We stopped *en route* for a cup of tea, then we stopped again later so that the kids could do what they should have done when we stopped earlier. Eventually we reached Dover, the kids chattering away excitedly at their first glimpse of the White Cliffs.

Checking in at the Hoverport was just a formality and took only a few minutes. We had decided to cross the Channel by hovercraft as it took only 35 minutes, an hour less than the ferry, and it would not only give us longer in France, it would be less time for the kids to be seasick. Happily the crossing was as smooth as glass and when we disembarked at Calais, it had stopped raining and the sun was peeping down at us through patches of blue sky. Most of the car passengers on our hovercraft were about to start on the long drive through France to the south – but not us. We were travelling by French Railways – car and all.

Several years ago, I too, used to drive all the way across France. But I found that, although going there was quite pleasant with the happy prospect of the holiday ahead, I came to dread the long drive back. One year I put the car on the train at Nice, booked myself a sleeper and from then on I was hooked. It's so simple, especially since French Railways have now introduced a daily Calais/Nice service which leaves the Gare Maritime at Calais at 7.20 p.m. every evening. It may take longer than flying but it's much cheaper, particularly when you add the cost of hiring a car. And as for driving all the way, when you've paid for your petrol, the motorway tolls and one overnight stop *en route* there's very little difference in price. The big advantage, of course, is that you step off the train rested and refreshed after a good night's sleep.

Now that we are all one, big, happy European family, going through Customs and Immigration is a piece of 'gâteau'. We were waved swiftly through and set off for the *'centre ville'* – the town centre. It is our custom to arrive in Calais every year in time to enjoy lunch at one of our favourite restaurants, 'Le Détroit' on the Boulevard de la Résistance. Luckily, there's hardly anything the children won't eat, so we never have a problem with the menu. However, on the debit side, they do have a passion for tomato ketchup – they put it on everything. *Moules marinières* and tomato ketchup caused a few French eyebrows to rise.

After lunch we all walked across the Pont Mobile to the beach – or rather, my wife and I walked – walking is something the children have never learned to do. They run everywhere, it tires me out just to watch them. The beach at Calais is very pleasant. There are games to occupy the children, and best of all, a bar where my wife and I can sit and enjoy a cognac. There are plenty of other things to do in Calais – the Cathédrale de Notre Dame is well worth a visit, as is the Monument des Bourgeois de Calais, or you can while away the time watching the locals playing the national game of boule in the Parc St Pierre.

Soon it was time to make our way back to the car and drive to the Gare Maritime. Our tickets were checked, we collected our *billets* for *petit déjeuner* the following morning, and watched as our car was loaded on the transporter which would soon be attached to the rear of the train. There was just enough time to call in at the station buffet and buy some sandwiches, a bottle of wine and a couple of orange drinks for us to consume on the train, before the train itself glided into the station. We climbed aboard the wagon-lit and found our sleeping compartments. We had booked two adjoining compartments, each containing two bunk-type single beds. While the kids had their customary argument about who was sleeping in which bed, I looked out of the window to the busy scene on the platform – some late arrivals, a few tears as people said *au revoir* to loved ones and a French family who had lost their tickets and couldn't remember which sleeper they were in.

Miraculously everything was quickly sorted out, the train pulled out of the station and we were on our way. We all sat by the window, eating our sandwiches and watching the French countryside passing by. Soon it grew dark and we tucked our by now sleepy kids in their beds, finished our bottle of wine and turned in ourselves.

I awoke just after 6.00 a.m. to find the train stopped at Marseilles. The sun shone down from a clear blue sky, and as I put my head out of the window, my nostrils were assailed by that familiar aroma of the south of France – a subtle combination of olives, mimosa, Gauloises and garlic. A little later we were served with breakfast – croissants, crispy rolls, jam and a huge mug of delicious, steaming coffee. We watched as the train hugged the coast, giving us delightful glimpses of golden beaches and a turquoise sea, and at 9.40 a.m., dead on time, the train pulled in to Nice. As we got off the train, that wonderful Mediterranean sunshine hit our sun-starved British skins. We walked across to the *quai d'autos* where our car would be unloaded. We were here at last. It had taken us just over 24 hours, but it had been fun all the way.

If you study the above article carefully, you will see that it fulfils all the conditions required of article writing. It is informative and, at the same time, entertaining. It's the type of article that could appeal to lots of magazines – *She, Reader's Digest, Signature,* to name but a few. Articles of this nature are not difficult to write as they are mainly based on a factual event or experience, but in developing your idea remember the following rules. Keep it short. Many inexperienced writers make the mistake of overwriting. Don't. Choose your words economically and your article will flow along and have much more pace. It's a great temptation sometimes to try and be too clever and too literary but quite often this leads to your article being long-winded and pompous. So stick to the point and don't wander away from your subject. Another important piece of advice is to construct your article so that it progresses smoothly from one point to the next. Plot it out before you start to write so that you know exactly where you are going. In other words, although it's an article, you should still look for a beginning, a middle and an end.

Short stories

Apart from the basic rules of deciding on a beginning, middle and an end, a very important point to bear in mind when you start to develop your idea more fully is not to fill your short story with too many characters. Too many characters only confuse the reader, who has enough to remember as it is. As you start to develop your idea it's a useful thing to jot down progressively the salient points of your story, so that you don't stray too far from the main theme. Again, beware of overwriting and filling your story with irrelevant material. Be descriptive. It's important to create a mood with which your reader can identify. Getting your reader in the right mood can greatly enhance your story. Consider the following passage from one of Edgar Allan Poe's classic horror stories:

> The forehead was high and very pale, and singularly placid; and the once jetty hair fell partially over it, and overshadowed the hollow temples with innumerable ringlets now of a vivid yellow, and jarring discordantly, in their fantastic character, with the reigning melancholy of the countenance. The eyes were lifeless and lustreless, and seemingly pupil-less, and I shrank involuntarily from their glassy stare to the contemplation of the thin and shrunken lips. They parted; and in a smile of peculiar meaning the teeth of the changed Berenice disclosed themselves slowly to my view. Would to God that I had never beheld them, or that, having done so, I had died.

You can see how Poe uses descriptive words to create a mood that slowly builds into an atmosphere of dread. Descriptive writing is very important in both short stories and novels. (In a play, either for radio or television, there is no place for descriptive writing. An atmosphere is created by visual and sound effects, and the tone of voice in which the actor delivers his or her lines.) The writer of fiction can choose words carefully to describe events and emotions, and make the reader feel happiness, sadness or fear. If your story is about two young people falling in love on holiday in Spain, make the reader feel he or she *is* in Spain. Describe the weather, the trees, the flowers. Tell the reader what the boy feels for the girl and what she feels for him. If you're writing an adventure story, make your reader feel part of the action. Try and create in the reader's mind the same attitudes and emotions experienced by the characters. If you can learn to do this then your story will come alive and grip the reader's imagination.

We've mentioned the love story, the crime story and adventure story, but these are just three of the many themes you may choose to develop. As you become more experienced, you will discover that a short story can spring from one simple idea, and if it's written well it doesn't always have to be built from a strong dramatic plot. Just read this – it's only very short but it shows what you can do with a simple idea and a bit of imagination.

NO PLACE LIKE HOME

He couldn't be anything other than English. Who but an Englishman would be found sitting in a deck chair on the beach in the south of France, in a temperature of nearly 80 degrees, wearing grey flannel trousers with braces, over a white, open-necked shirt and with a knotted handkerchief on his head.

He was from Bury in Lancashire, and he was in the middle of a fortnight's package tour which his wife had persuaded him to take against his better judgement.

He would have preferred Blackpool, where they had spent every August for the past twenty-eight years. Since the very first day they arrived, he'd done nothing but complain.

'What the 'eck's this?'

'Breakfast, dear.'

'Breakfast? Breakfast? I want more than a bit of cake for breakfast.'

'They call them croissants, dear.'

'I don't care what they call them. I want egg and bacon – like I always have!'

'They don't do them here, dear.'

'Bloody place! I told you we should have gone to Blackpool.'

'Yes, dear.'

He flatly refused to speak a word of French to anyone.

'They should speak English.'

'But they're French, dear.'

'Flaming foreigners!'

'No. We're the foreigners, dear.'

'Don't talk rubbish, woman. 'Ow can *we* be foreigners? We're English! They're the foreigners!'

'Yes, dear.'

He hated the hotel.

'Bloody twin beds!'

'Nice for a change.'

'I'm glad you think so. I can't sleep. I haven't slept a wink since we've come here.'

'You were snoring last night, dear.'

'No I wasn't! I was just breathing hard.'

'Yes, dear.'

He was bored out of his tiny, Lancashire mind.

'There's nothing to do, is there, except sit on the beach and look at the sea.'

'It's a nice view, dear.'

'When you've seen it once, you've seen it haven't you? I mean why don't they have bingo here? Or somewhere like the pleasure beach? You can't even get a decent drink.'

'I thought you liked the beer, dear.'

'Maiden's water!'

'Yes, dear.'

'Little and Large were on at the Central Pier this year.'

'You saw them last year, dear.'

'I like them.'

'Last year you said they were rubbish, dear.'

'I didn't.'

'No, dear. Whatever you say, dear.'

And so on, *ad infinitum*. Every day he found something else to complain about.

No *Coronation Street*.

Thin chips.

No mushy peas.

The price of a newspaper.

Under-done meat.

Weak tea.

No Mother's Pride.

Garlic.

No H.P. Sauce.

Etc . . . etc . . .

The first thing he did when they got back to Bury was to go out to his local pub for a pint of bitter and a meat pie.

And, do you know, the funny thing was, he never stopped telling everybody what a marvellous holiday he'd had.

The story you have just read was based entirely on observation and imagination. The man sitting on the beach in his grey flannel trousers and wearing the knotted handkerchief actually did exist. He, at least, was real. The rest was the result of the writer's fertile imagination. So you see how the most trivial of incidents can provide you with an idea to start your thought processes working.

But enough of that. It's time we moved on from the short story to something a little bit bigger.

The novel

The obvious difference between writing a short story and writing a novel is of course the length. A novel can be anything from 75 000 words upwards. It is for this reason that your idea and its subsequent development has to be far bigger than that required for a short story and contain much more in terms of story content and characterisation. Writing a novel is a difficult task, and one which we feel the new writer should not embark upon until he or she has had a considerable amount of writing experience. To write a novel will need more ingenuity and inventiveness, to say nothing of stamina. However, if you are optimistic enough to think you can do it – have a go. You'll still have to find a beginning, middle and end, and your idea will have to be big enough to sustain the reader's interest and attention for many pages.

Radio drama

The most important thing to remember when writing a play for radio is that you are creating sound pictures for your listener. In the previous chapter we have already discussed some of the advantages of writing a radio play – the fact that it can be set anywhere you wish and so on – but what you must not overlook is the value of sound effects. The right effects can create a sense of reality in your play. In a way, sound effects can take the place of descriptive writing, by helping to create the right mood – the wind whistling, the hooting of an owl, a creaking door can all help to create the right atmosphere for the listener. The use of music can also be very useful in helping to put the listener in the right frame of mind. A strong dramatic play can be enhanced by a piece of dramatic music, and soft violins will help set the right mood for your romantic play. In Chapter 5 we'll explain how you insert references for music into your script. The next time that you go to the cinema, just notice how the use of the right piece of music adds to your enjoyment of the film. We can't understand why it isn't used more on radio or television, but don't be afraid to suggest it.

Television drama

The one golden rule when developing an idea for a television play is to think visually. Always keep in mind the fact that when your characters speak your lines, they are seen to be speaking them. So you must visualise what they are doing. Are they sitting down, standing up, having a drink? You have to describe the action and use action to indicate to a director and the cast exactly how you wish your play to be interpreted. Always keep a mental picture of a television screen in your mind when developing your idea, and plot the idea within that frame. Look at your storyline. Go through it several times to see if it's visual enough. Is there another way to do a particular scene so that it becomes more visually interesting?

A conversation between two characters may have much more visual impact if it takes place in a pub, or on a park bench, rather than in a kitchen.

If you are intending to submit your finished synopsis to the BBC then it must have a beginning, middle and end. However, if you are going to submit it to one of the Independent Television companies, then you need to take into consideration that in an hour's play there will be two commercial breaks. So, as well as your beginning, middle and end, you will need to construct your play to allow for these. When you start to develop your play you must think of two suitable moments in it, where the two commercial breaks can be placed. These moments should be ones that leave the viewer wondering what is going to happen next – they're known in the business as 'cliff-hangers' and are meant to keep the viewer tuned to that particular television channel. You should indicate in your storyline exactly where you wish the commercial breaks to occur. But a word of caution. Should you submit an idea to an Independent Television company and it is rejected, and you then decide to send it to the BBC, make sure you delete all references to commercial breaks. Some BBC producers can be quite touchy about being second thoughts.

Films

Developing an idea for a film is not dissimilar to developing a television play. You need a beginning, middle and end, and you must think in visual terms. The main difference is that for the big screen you need a really big idea. You have none of the restrictions which television imposes: limited location filming, only so many studio sets. With a film the scope is limitless, and the only restriction is to keep within the budget. However, we should point out that most screenplays are commissioned and the chances of an unsolicited film script being picked up by a Steven Spielberg or David Puttnam is rarer than finding a snowman in the Sahara.

Stage plays

Writing for the stage has its own peculiar problems; as we discussed earlier, the main one is that most plays, whether a comedy or a drama, normally have only one set, so your idea must be one that can be played within one set. Also, when developing your idea, bear in mind that your finished play will have at least one interval, if not two, so that you must provide one or two 'cliff-hangers' to make sure the audience returns from the bar for the start of the next act.

Summing up

Well, that's about it as far as 'idea development' is concerned, but before you move on, remember:

1 Find a good end and a good beginning before you start to develop the middle.
2 Don't forget conflict, suspense, pathos and humour.
3 Originality is better than *déjà vu*.
4 Be entertaining.

You're probably wondering when we're going to get round to the actual business of writing. Be patient. There's a lot more that you need to know before you start sharpening your pencils.

4. Character

Why do actors weep with delight when they are offered the part of Shylock in Shakespeare's *The Merchant of Venice*?

The answer is **Character!**

Why has Harold Brighouse's play *Hobson's Choice* become a classic example of theatre and film work?

The answer is **Character!**

And why is the name of Scrooge attributed to anyone who is mean?

The answer, yet again, is **Character!**

Character, when writing fiction, is all-important. To drum this lesson home, we would like to illustrate how a play or story might have failed had the character drawing been weak and indecisive. You may point out that some of these creations were based on real people. True, but we are talking about how they have been successfully fictionalised. Read, mark, learn and inwardly digest, because you, too, should learn to write characters as well-drawn and clearly defined as these.

Without Captain Bligh there would have been no *Mutiny on the Bounty*. He was dogmatic, domineering, bullying and sadistic – in fact, due to the success of the original film, he was the 'man we loved to hate'. He was also a strict disciplinarian. Just think, without him there is no story.

Without Jeeves, P. G. Wodehouse's famous butler, there would have been no Bertie Wooster stories. Horrifying, we know, because everyone loves silly ass Bertie, but Bertie on his own isn't strong enough to carry the fiction – he needs the strength of Jeeves behind him, to take him through his inevitable crisis and make the important decisions for him. Even though Jeeves emerges only now and again, he is the strength behind the stories. He doesn't walk, he 'shimmers'. And when Jeeves wants to get his own way, he gets it, no matter what opposition the 'young master' puts in his way. There is nobody in this world who could cause a briefer and more pregnant silence than a Jeeves, who, although not actually disgruntled, is 'far from being gruntled'. A masterpiece of characterisation, but only to be expected from the great Wodehouse. If you haven't already made Jeeves' acquaintance, don't waste any more time. Make it now.

And our third shining example comes in Margaret Mitchell's *Gone With The Wind*. Scarlett O'Hara and Rhett Butler seem to keep that story alive, particularly Scarlett, who dominates both book and film. Scarlett's character is so strong that she seems to have an effect on just about everyone, men *and* women. No one is safe from Scarlett. She is supremely egotistical, wayward, headstrong, vain and beautiful. She exploits every situation to the full; and every time she meets someone, although she may be outwardly making polite platitudes, you can almost hear her saying, 'What's in it for me?'

Her main problem is that she cannot make up her mind – or at least, not for long. The grass is always greener on the other side for Scarlett, and even at the end when Rhett finally leaves her, you know that if he had stayed she'd have thought of something or someone else tomorrow.

A chameleon of a character, but so well drawn that Margaret Mitchell must have had a wonderful time writing her.

Looking for characters

Character is important to all of us, but especially to writers. When you meet somebody, you either remember them or forget them. If you remember them it is usually something about them – their character – that stays in your mind. If you don't remember them it is probably because they are bland. That is, they are reticent, shy, retiring or unimpressive. They remain unnoticed, and the last thing you would wish about your writing is that it should remain unnoticed.

Charles Dickens was a master of characterisation, creating many characters who came to life, and for him, all his observation of people reaped rich dividends. His books were really based on his characters, tied together by a theme. 'Ah, yes,' you may say, 'that's all very well, but you're showing us established characters, characters that have already been written and recognised. Fair enough, but what about new characters? They don't grow on trees. Where d'you find them?'

They're all around you. We've just mentioned the magic word

'observation' and that sums it up. Look at yourself for a start. To another writer, you *are* a character. You react in certain ways to certain occurrences, you have mannerisms that may or may not infuriate other people and you think in a certain way. You're a character all right, and so is everyone else. Look around you. Observe your friends. Develop 'character awareness'.

Character is what makes people tick. In the main, we all react differently to the same situation. Some people act straight away without thinking, whilst others sit on the fence. Others want to think about it before they act. Let's take a dramatic situation and put three people in it.

A train has crashed and there are three people in a particular carriage, two men and a woman. The carriage doors have jammed and the people are stuck. Perhaps the carriage is tilted slightly, so there is a fear that it might overbalance altogether; and there is another worry – fire! Three passengers, all in the same situation, and having to wait until help from outside arrives. How will they react?

We asked a class of 25 writing students how they would behave in a similar situation and although some agreed that they would react in the same way, you'd be surprised how many varying reactions we discovered.

Some of them said they'd be terrified, some said that they'd calm themselves and wait till help arrived, and others were extremely practical, examining ways to wrench things (fittings and so on) from the walls of the carriage so they could try to break the windows with these. Of course, the students were all fit and well, and they weren't actually *in* the carriage, which made an obvious difference, but if, for instance, you took someone, man or woman, who had just come out of hospital after a mental illness and put that person into the carriage, you've got a different story. And as a situation develops, so a character may change. What begins as complacency can develop into fear, which may affect the others.

Let's take another situation which, these days, seems to be becoming all too commonplace. Imagine you work in a bank. At a couple of minutes to closing time, the bank is held up, and you are the one who is confronted by the gunman and told to hand over the money. What would you do? Would you try to talk him out of it, as one young bank cashier did – with success – would you hand it over without a murmur, or would you try to press the button giving the alarm? In the past, people have also tried to tackle the robbers and got hurt for their trouble. It all depends on the character of the cashier. Then, of course, there are the customers in the bank. Perhaps one of them would try to help the cashier. It all depends on the character of the customer.

To give your characters flesh and blood when you write about them, and by 'write' we mean describe them, you need to know them. You must have a detailed picture in your own mind in order to be able to describe them for your readers. Most writers base part of their character writing on someone they know, or someone they've met or seen; someone who has impressed them, and this is where character awareness comes in, improving your observation and knowing what you are looking for.

As in Chapter 2, when we talked about observing people in buses, trains, supermarkets and so on to seed ideas in your mind, you will need to develop the same awareness to help with your character drawing. For a start, you must acknowledge the fact that nobody sees everything. There is always something overlooked, and if you can supply this missing ingredient your character will take off in your mind and impress itself on other people. If you can create something a little different in your character, you will find a way to giving that character an unusual reaction and perhaps something different to say – all of which makes the characterisation more vivid.

On this important subject of observation, the French writer Flaubert gave some valuable advice to another up-and-coming French writer, Guy de Maupassant:

> In everything [writes Flaubert] there is still some spot unexplored, because we are accustomed only to use our eyes with the recollection of what others before us have thought on the same subject. The smallest object contains something unknown.
>
> When you pass a grocer seated at his shop door, a janitor smoking his pipe, a stand of hackney carriages, show me that grocer and that janitor – their attitude, their whole physical appearance, so that I cannot confound them with any other grocer or janitor; make me see that a certain cab-horse does not resemble the fifty others that follow or precede it.

Valuable advice indeed! What others don't see, you can see if you look for it, so study your fellows. Look for the little things, the idiosyncracies that will distinguish your character from all the others dreamed up since fiction began. Just because another writer has written a story about a wealthy banker doesn't mean that you can't and that yours won't be different. You must see the character you are about to describe very clearly in your imagination so that the reader will be able to see the very same person. After all, that person exists only in your mind, and you and your writing will be the reader's only link with him.

Like 'idea awareness', practise 'character awareness' and you'll find that looking for characters in your routine life can be fun. In time your observation will become more and more acute, and your characters more varied.

You need time to develop characters, which is why they belong more in novels, plays and lengthier short stories. In the average short story these days, which generally has a length of 1200–1500 words, time and words are precious, and so the accent tends to be on action more than character building. Your characters will have names and occupations, and if the story idea is strong enough with sufficient conflict, pace, suspense and a twist ending to follow, the reader will often not need to know much more. Occasionally, naturally, a short story built around character is written, often in the first person, in which case you have time to examine the character and motivation in detail, but for the reader with ten minutes to spare you will usually go for a pacey story with lots happening and an ending which tries to keep one jump ahead of the reader (the sting in the tail).

We will discuss the advantages of writing in the first and third person later in this chapter, but for the moment, it's back to character.

You will find in many cases that when you begin to write lines for your characters they are lines dreamed up by you, the writer. Now that seems a silly thing to say, doesn't it? On the face of it, it is stupid! Naturally the writer writes the lines for the characters. Who else writes them – the characters themselves?

Prepare for a shock. The answer is – yes! in a roundabout way.

If you know your characters sufficiently well, you will find that they gradually come to have minds of their own. You will find that the more you develop and write them, you and the characters become as one, and suddenly you're not the writer any more. You're the interpreter of their thoughts. You are putting down on paper for them what they want to do and what they want to say.

We know this sounds spooky, but it's true. The characters take you over, and the times when you sat back, looked at your sheet of paper in the typewriter and thought 'What can Harold say to that'

are over. You won't have to think about it. You will know immediately what Harold would say and write it. You will find that the
dialogue comes automatically – but only if your characters are
right, and if you get inside them. You must forget that you are the
writer and become part of the characters. You will then find that
the lines are natural lines instead of stagey, wooden lines, and that
they'll flow easily. At the beginning, before you've learned to do
this, you'll find it's hard work, and, as some kind publisher, producer or critic will tell you, your characters are interchangeable. If
the lines *are* interchangeable, then you haven't worked out your
characters properly.

Give your characters a purpose, a reason for being there in the
first place, and a point of view which the others can react to, and
you have something and someone to write about. If you don't,
then you'll be struggling, because you really have nothing to say.

Remember what we told you originally, that everyone is a character and we are all different in certain respects. The face doesn't
always tell you the nature of the person behind it. Trusting someone can bring you a nasty and unexpected shock. Just when you
are relying on good old George for his backing he lets you down.
Remember these things. They will help you when it comes to
building your own major characters.

If you have created an hypnotic hero, or a villain hated by
everyone, you have done your job well. Glenn Chandler, the
Scottish writer, did a wonderful character building job in the
police television series *Taggart*. The main characters of Taggart
and his young assistant officer stand out, and to a lesser extent, so
does his long-suffering wife. Taggart is an anti-hero; seldom
smiling, but sometimes allowing the merest suggestion of one to
wrinkle his mouth. Terse and firm of purpose, he goes on his way
allowing nothing to block the path to justice, and the conviction of
a killer. But you feel that behind the implacable face is a kind man,
and this makes you like him, keeping you always on the look-out
for that hint of humour. And when it comes, you're happy.

The assistant (he's already had a couple so far) bounces off his
boss nicely. Although he is occasionally put in his place by
Taggart in a very headmasterly way, you feel that he doesn't really
object to it and respects and admires Taggart. He sometimes tries
to get one jump ahead, but is never allowed the last word.

Taggart's wheelchair-bound wife always seems to be waiting
for him to come home at a certain time and, of course, he seldom
does. For her, the word long-suffering is an understatement. His

dinner is usually cold when he eats it, and although the unemotional Taggart tries to explain the 'whys and wherefores' to her in as few words as possible, we can see by her reticent manner that she realises all too late that she is part of a Policeman's Lot. She knows that his job comes first with Taggart; his task of protecting the public matters more to him than does arriving home on time to attend his own anniversary party. Hers is not a large role but it is an important one, carefully written, and just like that of the young Sergeant, it is not only complete in itself, but also explains more about Taggart's character.

We hope that this analysis enables you to read more into character composition than is obvious on the surface. Which seems to have taken us neatly into the question of writing character for the different mediums, but as we are talking television, we'll stay with it.

The next time you watch something as professionally excellent as *Taggart*, don't simply look at the overall picture, look at the character drawing, and see how this helps to subsidise the story content. Although it may have started as a tough crime series, it is now also the story of a man – Taggart. As television is a visual medium it helps that your audience is able to see your characters. However, what they *can't* see is what lies beneath the exterior.

Before you begin writing you should have done a certain amount of planning so you know what you are going to write about and how your piece will be constructed. If you've done this, you should also know the nature of the people in it. You should know how they are going to react to the situation in which you have cunningly placed them. You should know how they tick. If you have done your homework and worked out a background for them – their home, their office, their club, their family, friends and even enemies, you should know what kind of people they are and who you are writing about. This being so, you have also decided how they speak, and what their views on life will be. If you've reached this point, then you are ready to start. You are about to write about human beings, not cardboard characters. And if you've got inside your character, he or she will speak exactly the way you want them to in your dialogue, which we'll be coming to very shortly.

When you write for radio, you will need to have done the same homework for your characters. Radio being all about words, however, with not an actor in sight, the dialogue is even more important – in a radio play it is everything. You mustn't forget that the words are the listener's only link with what is going on in your play. Your words must tell him or her everything he or she needs to know. Your words must tell him or her who is speaking, what they are doing, where they are going and why, who is speaking to whom – the lot!

Simply remember, with your characterisation for radio, that it must all be indicated with words. If she is lazy, it must be referred to; if he is ruthless, we must have someone to tell us that he is ruthless; every characteristic, even that a character walks with a limp, must be pointed out. But character must be just as carefully thought out in radio as in every other medium.

The short story on radio, *Morning Story*, for example, is very much akin to the short story in print, except that it is read aloud by an actor instead of being read silently at home. A character is presented in narrative form. You may describe the appearance of your character – short, thick-set, close-cropped hair, or however you want that person to be – so that the reader/listener has an image to bear in mind. That is the 'descriptive' side of character writing, but the characters' inner selves will emerge bit by bit as the plot progresses, and gradually as the conflict grows. And we do mean gradually. Don't try to show a character all at once, as some new writers do. Let us learn about them slowly. Just because your main character may have had a nervous breakdown and ended up in hospital, we don't need to know about the electrical treatment, reserved for the most serious patients, unless it is going to affect the story or plot. If that is so, then let us hear about it when necessary, and retain some surprises. We all thought that the main character sounded a little odd at the beginning of the story, so keep us in suspense as to why for a little longer. Don't blurt it all out at the beginning, otherwise you won't be able to produce a new surprise in the place that matters. Just give some background, enough to intrigue us and suggest that something riveting is going to happen in the very near future. This feeds the reader/listener's imagination and gives the much-needed sense of anticipation that every story needs. It keeps the momentum up and every development of a character's background which affects the movement of the story will help to make the reader want to see what is going to happen next.

Character and plots

Before we finish with character, there is one other important facet to be discussed. It not only plays a vital part in all work of length and value, but can sometimes be the instigator of the plot or story; the characters 'create' their own plots.

We have already talked about idea awareness for plot fertilisation. Some writers even start with a title and get their story from that, but many get their basic ideas from their characters; that is, the story will grow out of the particular characters you have in mind.

If you have a main character, for instance, who has an enquiring, not to say inquisitive, mind, it could be that this curiosity begins a chain of events.

A private eye, such as Raymond Chandler's Philip Marlowe, is approached by his clients because of his incisive mind. Marlowe was also, however, particularly susceptible to the wrong type of lady and was often beaten up several times during the story because of this. Other 'eyes' cruised through their stories, only getting beaten up as necessary, but with Marlowe, it was generally because of the 'beautiful broads'. And he never learned!

The American writer, Thorne Smith, had a series of major characters, all of whom had basically the same inherent quality of sadness. Although his books were wildly funny at times, the hero, and occasionally the heroine, were sad people. They wanted to be happy, yet were not.

His 'Topper' character was an example. A mild little man who simply wanted to live and let live, Topper was dominated by his wife and longed for happiness. This he obtained through George and Marion Kerby, two young people who lived it up. Then one day, they crashed their car into a tree, died, and came back to 'liven up' Topper's dreary life by 'materialising' and 'dematerialising' and leading Topper into the most outrageous adventures. This led to a very successful series of books and films. Sadness, boredom and being misunderstood were the sole qualities of Thorne Smith's heroes, and the reason why all his books were escapist. His heroes wanted to 'get away from it all', and, one suspects, so did Thorne Smith. We feel sorry for Topper, but study the character writing – real life indeed, beautifully observed.

> Topper watched his wife remove her sewing-glasses and place them in their case. With an absorbed gaze he followed her movements as she folded her sewing and wrapped it in a piece of linen, which she then deposited in a basket. At this point his expression became desperate, then hopeless.

Although we will be dealing with situation comedy for radio and television in other chapters, we feel that a look at one of America's most important television characters of recent times – well, since the 1950s – fits in well here. We refer to Master Sergeant Ernest Bilko.

Bilko's series, originally entitled *You'll Never Get Rich*, was about trying to become rich and never quite succeeding. The series was about this because this is what Bilko was all about. The character of Bilko was the instigator of the series, a supreme example of what we are talking about, how character creates plot.

Bilko, like Topper, wanted to escape from his humdrum existence, but in a different manner. Topper had money and Bilko didn't, but Bilko wanted it. He thought that money, lots of it, would buy him happiness. Bilko's character was brilliantly well-drawn. When you least expected it you would find that underneath the hard, conniving exterior he had a streak of sentimentality. In one episode he would come to the rescue of Private Doberman who had had all his money conned from him by card sharps – in another he would save his Commanding Officer, Colonel Hall, from falling into disgrace with High Command in Washington. But the main aim of the series was Bilko's efforts to acquire wealth – how to raise it by running dances; buying a racehorse and training it on the camp at night to win a big race; entering choral concerts with his platoon; conning film star Bing Crosby to be guest star at a camp concert for charity (Bilko's), and so on.

Again, next time they are re-run, watch the programmes to see how the Bilko character motivates the stories and the action. See how Nat Hiken, who devised the series, and the writers 'think' Bilko. They get inside the character. You can see them saying to each other 'What would *Bilko* do here?' – not 'What shall *we* do here?' There's a total difference. Bilko's thinking, planning and scheming belonged only to the Bilko mind. This is what you must do with your characters. 'Think' the character. Become the character. It works!

Dialogue and character

We feel that no one can take everything in at once, which is why we repeat things now and again – but only important things. Repetition ensures that the little detail you've forgotten is once again back in mind, and helps you to remember it.

Also, you will have realised by now that so many aspects of creative writing are interlinked. Time and time again, questions of characterisation come up in different forms, and it is here again when we consider dialogue. We repeat 'Think out your characters properly. If you don't, you're in trouble, and you will find your dialogue hard work.' Plot, too, goes hand-in-hand with dialogue and character, and many people, thinking that plot is necessary but dull, try to get it across far too quickly.

Nothing could be more ill-conceived. Plot is very important – it is, after all, what your entire story, script or play is hanging on

To put a résumé of past action over in one large lump in dialogue is a mistake, especially if a good deal of it is sketching in a background. It becomes boring, because generally you have one character telling one or more other characters all about himself, his family, his background before he met them and so on. The other character(s) simply nod and all you get is one person's point of view with nothing coming from anyone else. This becomes a yawn. Take the following example. It is from a very good play by Jill Woods, called *The Birthday Boy*. The family are gathered round at the funeral reception of Hugh's late wife, Phyllis. Margaret, who is Ted's wife and Phyllis' sister-in-law, is holding forth on how she and Ted heard the news. If we cut out Ted's interpolations – which we are going to do – the speech seems to go on and on. After this example, we will give you the same speech, but this time broken up by Ted's remarks. These not only allow Margaret to give her views, but cleverly allow us to see the relationship between her and Ted, in a way which other people wouldn't normally see.

MARGARET   We couldn't believe it! Ted and I just couldn't believe it! We were just setting out for Torquay when we heard. It put a blight on the whole holiday. I mean, if she'd been knocked down by a bus or something we would have been shocked! But to go like *that*! You just can't plan for anything like *that*, can you Ted? We just didn't know whether to unpack all the suitcases or what, did we? In the end we went, just for five days. Having a motor caravan, you're your own boss – do what you like. We got back yesterday, in time for today. Felt almost guilty, enjoying ourselves in the sun. I mean, she's no relation to me, just Ted's sister-in-law, but we

still felt guilty. Didn't we, Ted? We didn't enjoy
ourselves . . . well, *I* did . . . in a way – you know
what I mean. Life goes on . . . and we had
wonderful weather . . . (CHEWS SANDWICH) . . .
Mmmm. You know, I do think they might have
chosen a different filling . . . you know, not fish
paste.

We'll stop there. Now the actress has to be good indeed to carry
on like that, endlessly and still retain attention. But if you break it
up a little:

MARGARET   We couldn't believe it! Ted and I just couldn't
             believe it! We were just setting out for Torquay
             when we heard. It put a blight on the whole
             holiday. I mean, if she'd been knocked down by
             a bus or something, we would have been
             shocked – but to go like *that*! You just can't plan
             for anything like *that*, can you Ted?
TED   (MECHANICALLY) Out of the blue, Margaret.
             Couldn't believe it.
MARGARET   We just didn't know whether to unpack all the
             suitcases or what, did we? In the end we went,
             just for five days. Having a motor caravan,
             you're your own boss – do what you like. We got
             back yesterday, in time for today.
             Felt almost guilty, enjoying ourselves in the sun.
             I mean, she's no relation to me, just Ted's sister-
             in-law, but we still felt guilty. Didn't we, Ted?
TED   We didn't enjoy ourselves, did we?
MARGARET   Oh *I* did . . . well, in a way – you know what I
             mean. Life goes on . . . and we had *wonderful*
             weather . . .
TED   (BORED) Do you want another sandwich?
MARGARET   Mmmm. You know, I do think they might have
             chosen a different filling . . . you know, not fish
             paste.
TED   She choked on a fish *bone*, not a fish paste
             sandwich!
MARGARET   I know she did, but all the same . . .

You can see how Ted's lines create a more complete picture of
Margaret and Margaret and Ted. We can see who wears the
trousers in that household, and we can see how Ted puts up with

Margaret and probably gets his happiest leisure hours in the pub with his friends. Just that little extra thought behind your dialogue and you give a much more complete character picture. Ted's lines also show more about Margaret than her own lines reveal. They show that she is always like this, in any sort of company in any situation, or on any occasion. The lesson plainly is take your time over your plot laying. Let all the characters have a say in things. Let them take part in it, let them react or give their opinions. As long as they are saying something or contributing to the story in some way, it is all valuable. In this way you will develop both plot and character at the same time.

After all, plot and story line are vital ingredients; they are the reason the story starts and finishes. Never try to rush them.

A final example of dialogue from Jill Woods' play *The Birthday Boy*. The funeral reception we read earlier was for Hugh's wife, Phyllis. We haven't heard about the 'real' Phyllis up to now. In the following dialogue, this emerges gradually and humorously showing us something about Hugh too. He has met up with an old friend, Dick, in a local pub and they have a heart to heart.

HUGH   Glad to see a couple of old faces. I missed the old place, you know. Never thought I would.

DICK   Reciprocated, I believe. Your successor's running Annuities like an army training camp. Can't keep a secretary for more than two weeks.

HUGH   Ha! Well, they said I lacked fire.

DICK   Self-motivation, that's the name of the game now. An ability to step over crushed bodies on your way to the top. I didn't think you'd miss the rat race.

HUGH   Well, it wasn't like I planned, really. Didn't end up doing the things I thought I would – and wanted to!

DICK   You're not the only one. Tell me about her, Hugh.

HUGH   Well . . .

DICK   Nothing stopping you now.

HUGH   No. (PAUSES) It's a funny thing, retirement. Stay in and you're always under her feet. (WRYLY) And Phyllis had size eights! You feel . . . discarded. Have to keep busy, if you can.

DICK   And you haven't?

HUGH   (WISTFULLY) A trip to the Seychelles, I thought. Maybe more than one holiday. And the whole garden landscaped. It wouldn't have broken us. She was

always . . . very . . . careful with money. I couldn't see
the objections.

DICK   Which were?

HUGH   Hi-jacks, as far as holidays were concerned. No more
aeroplanes – ever. Even Brighton was suspect after the
bomb blast. And the garden – well, she didn't want it
changed. So last year we had a week in Hastings and I
bought a new gnome for the fish pond. (THOUGHTFUL)
We nearly came to blows over that gnome.

DICK   She was in the Territorial Army once, wasn't she?

HUGH   Yes. Always had a . . . regimental streak.
(REFLECTIVELY) She picked me up in the Underground,
you know, during an air raid. I used to say that was
the day I met my Waterloo, but over the years it wore
a bit thin, that joke. (THOUGHTFULLY) That was the only
time I ever remember her being frightened.

DICK   Mmmm, hard to associate Phyllis and fear. I would
have thought she'd even have scared off the
Luftwaffe!

HUGH   (WITH ADMIRATION) You should have seen her with
double-glazing salesmen. She could see them off with
a look, hardly a word spoken. Better than having a
guard dog, sometimes. (CHECKS HIMSELF) Still, I
shouldn't be . . .

DICK   Wrong. It needs saying.

HUGH   Not here to defend herself, is she?

DICK   You wouldn't be saying it if she was.

HUGH   No. I wouldn't dare.
THEY BOTH LAUGH

Note the natural, easy flow of the dialogue; of the man-to-man sympathy and gentle probing from Dick, and the wistful 'what a life I've
had' attitude from Hugh; and the revelations about Phyllis' character.
Nice, warm and constrained writing.

First or third person?

Whether to write in the first or third person often causes a debate.

Writing in the first person is writing as if the event had happened to you personally and it has both advantages and disadvantages.

The advantages are that the writing all sounds direct, even true, and has a sense of conviction about it. The disadvantages, unfortunately, outweigh the advantages. A character who describes his or her own adventures in the first person is always looking in a straight line, and will only be aware of his or her own thoughts and ideas. S/he has no idea what happens to the other people in the story when they leave, or s/he leaves them. This is very constraining for the writer.

The writer employing the third person, however, is able to be completely detached, unshackled by time and place. S/he views everyone from afar, and knows exactly what they're all doing or about to do any time or anywhere. S/he is able to describe every character, good or bad, in precise detail, and present their past, present and future. S/he has a completely free hand in writing the story as s/he knows what everyone is thinking.

If you're a beginner, it is far safer to write in the third person, as it will present you with less difficulties. It is a much more straight-forward way of handling a narrative. If you have a story to tell, then tell it. That is the important thing.

Summing up

1 Character is all around you, in you, in your friends and every-one you meet. Observe them and make notes.
2 Character can change with a situation – for example, your so-called reliable friend can let you down.
3 Give your characters flesh and blood. Get inside your charac-ters. Think and act like them, and you won't need to think up lines for them to say, *they*'ll put the words into *your* mouth.
4 Character breeds plot and story ideas.
5 Don't try to get your story or plot over in a solid wodge of text. Bring it out gradually and naturally in your dialogue.
6 Writing in the third person is the easier way for a new writer.

We have said that character pops up everywhere. It does, espe-cially in the next chapter on writing for radio.

5. Writing for Radio

We have both spent many happy hours writing for radio. In fact, that's how we started. Radio writing is, however, a specialist form of writing. You have to study the medium thoroughly to find out how it is done, and what it is all about.

As we have already mentioned, radio is the medium of the ear. You can't see what is happening on radio, you can only hear about it, and so everything has to be explained in words. The listeners must know everything that is going on, otherwise they are lost.

You, the writer must answer all those questions. Who is speaking? Who is being spoken to? Where are they? What do they plan to do? Where are they going? And so on. It's up to you to conjure up these pictures for the listeners so that they, too, can enjoy your mental images. They make up their own minds about what the characters look like, for instance (the actors and actresses seldom resemble the picture in the listeners' minds). This is why the enormously successful radio family, *The Glums*, were a flop on television. The cast, no matter how good they were, could never look like the characters people had imagined, originally played by Jimmy Edwards, June Whitfield and Dick Bentley.

In other words, the listeners had all built their own mental pictures of the Glums, based on the characters' voices and dialogue, and to try to match these with real people was asking for trouble.

Another example of 'listener thinking' occurred when HMS *Troutbridge* of *The Navy Lark*, starring Jon Pertwee, Leslie Phillips and Stephen Murray, was sailing the radio waves. Each Sunday night Joanna Murray, wife of Stephen Murray who played the part of Commander Murray, used to join the studio audience for the recordings. Once in the studio, she would sit back and close her eyes, not opening them again until the show was over. Joanna said that she, too, had her own personal image of the *Troutbridge* crew, and didn't want to spoil her enjoyment by watching the cast physically acting out the roles.

This shows you how vital words are to radio. Radio transports you to another world, and one of your own making at that. You must think in words and sound, and not until you do that will you succeed as a radio writer.

Yes, we did say 'words and sound'. By sound, we mean sound effects. Sound effects bring the action to life, so that a listener can take in what is happening and be a part of it.

Sound effects

The store of sound effects available these days is vast. You can have literally any sound you want, from a door opening and closing to Vesuvius erupting. In one episode of *The Navy Lark* the entire British Home Fleet collided with each other, ship by ship, and the result was hilarious and impressive, to say the least.

The BBC in particular have an enviable library of sound effects, and if by some outside chance they don't have the effect you want, they will make it up for you, as in the aforementioned home fleet collision.

When the Goons were at their peak, Spike Milligan made sound effects a feature of the show. The ones he asked for were outlandish, bizarre and prolonged and extended the Beeb Effects team to their limit, but they managed it. The result was a tower of extra laughs.

As we have already mentioned, in radio, unlike television, you are uninhibited by the number of sets available or the costs of location shooting. When you write for radio the world is yours – the spoken word can take the listener anywhere, even for the space of a few seconds.

Sometimes a narrator is used for setting up and establishing scenes, but the best radio script is usually the one which doesn't depend on devices like this, and in which everything emerges gradually from the dialogue.

Music is also used to create mood and atmosphere, and together with sound effects can improve the enjoyment of a programme enormously. Both are a bonus for the writer – and the listener! To indicate music you simply type the word GRAMS: just like that, in capital letters, and say what sort of music you want. For sound effects, type the word TAPE or F/X, and opposite it, give details of the effects you want.

However, first things come first, and here, the first thing is how your script is set out.

Presentation

It is important to present your work as neatly as possible. If a script unit sees a tatty-looking script inside the envelope, they will think that the writing is as careless as the presentation and shy away from it. The more professional the presentation looks, the sooner the script will get read. The BBC asks for manuscripts to be typed on A4 paper, and only on one side.

On the left-hand side of the page you type the scene number in capital letters. Underneath it, you type the information as to whether the scene takes place inside or outside – INTERIOR or EXTERIOR – and whether it takes place during the day or night.

This is how it should look on your page.

SCENE 1.
EXTERIOR. NIGHT.

Opposite this, spaced accordingly, comes the description of what particular effects you want for your scene. Like this:

SCENE 1.   (HIGH WIND WITH BLUSTERING RAIN. A CAR
EXTERIOR. NIGHT.   APPROACHES AT SPEED.)

Underneath this scene, time and effects setting, comes your dialogue, spaced appropriately as follows:

SCENE 1.   (HIGH WIND WITH BLUSTERING RAIN. A CAR
EXTERIOR. NIGHT.   APPROACHES AT SPEED.)

BOB   (SHOUTS) Tim! Lookout!
(LONG, SCREECHING SKID FOLLOWED BY A LOUD CRASH. SILENCE FOR A
FEW SECONDS EXCEPT FOR THE RAIN BEATING DOWN)
BOB   Tim . . . ? Tim, you all right?
TIM   (GROANS.)

Writing the play

That is how you present your play to the radio drama departments. Next comes the difficult bit, that of writing your play, complete with dialogue, sound effects and music.

Up to now, we've bent your ears to the importance of the spoken word on radio, and how radio depends on words to explain the who, where, when, why and how of it all to the listener; how music helps you to set a mood or an atmosphere, and how effects can help you to describe a scene in sound. But you would be surprised and amazed if you were asked to read some of the scripts that have been submitted to us, where events which should have been described in dialogue and effects have been described in visual terms. So you see, until you *really* know how, it can still be difficult.

For instance, one lady student we knew had her main character alone in her lounge on a very hot afternoon. She decided to go upstairs and have a bath to cool her down, and this was how the student described the action:

(CATHY PATS HER CAT, GOES OUT OF THE LOUNGE AND UPSTAIRS. SHE GOES INTO THE BATHROOM, TURNS ON THE HOT TAP AND UNDRESSES. THEN SHE GETS INTO THE BATH AND PICKS UP HER BOOK.)

We can only emphasise that the listener can't *see* her patting her cat, going up the stairs, turning on the hot tap, undressing, getting into the bath and picking up her book.

That is an actual example, so we're not being facetious. Until you know what radio writing is all about, you will find that either you make mistakes like that, or at the very least, stop and wonder how on earth you are going to do the next bit in dialogue. Well, let's see how it could be done . . .

In the play just quoted, Cathy was on her own, so to convey the action above she would have to keep on talking to herself – not to be recommended unless it is absolutely vital, and even then, it should be kept to the minimum. After all, none of us have terribly long conversations with ourselves. It isn't natural. Certainly we utter occasional words like 'Oh God, that's *all* I need!' but we don't go on about it. Anyway, we don't recommend this procedure, or you will end up with a sort of contrived monologue where Cathy has to explain to the listeners in as off-hand a way as possible that it is a very hot day, she has a cat, and is about to take a bath to cool her down. Something like this (the scene number has already been set, and we know that the scene is an interior one):

CATHY   (TO HERSELF) My word! I do feel like a bath. I think I'll have one! God! It's hot! And I think I'll take my book into the bathroom too, so I can read it in the bath. (TO CAT) Oh well, Tiddles, I must love you and leave you, so it's up those old stairs to the bathroom!
(FOOTSTEPS GOING UPSTAIRS.)

CATHY   Here we are in the bathroom. Now I'll turn on the hot
             tap . . . (WATER RUNNING INTO BATH.)
CATHY   Mmmm, that looks good. Now I'll get undressed. First
             I'll take off my . . .

But no! We won't go any further than that, but you can see what
we mean. It *is* contrived, isn't it? If you were going to get into a hot
bath, would *you* keep on speaking to yourself like that? Of course
you wouldn't! But what can you do to avoid all that? It's very
simple, really.

It's also blatant. You either have someone else in the lounge at
the start – neighbour, husband, friend, it doesn't matter who – or
you use a device, like a phone call. For example:

             (THE SOUND OF RUNNING WATER. THE PHONE RINGS.)
CATHY   Oh damn!
             (FOOTSTEPS ACROSS PARQUET FLOORING. PHONE UP.)
CATHY   Hello?
SYLVIA   (DISTORT) Cathy, darling. Sylvia!
CATHY   Sylvia, I'll ring you back! I've got the water running for a
             bath. Must rush or it'll be all over the floor. Speak to you
             soon!
             (PHONE DOWN. FOOTSTEPS ON PARQUET FLOORING.)
CATHY   Let's see . . .
             (WATER TURNED OFF.)
CATHY   Oooh! Just right! In we . . .oooh . . . lovely . . .
             (WATER SWIRLING GENTLY. A FEW SPLASHES.)
CATHY   (SIGHS LUXURIOUSLY) Now then, where was I? (GIGGLES)
             What a lovely title . . . *I Was A Slave To The Sultan Of
             Pasha*

Naturally we do sometimes speak to ourselves but generally
these are muttered asides. You have to get across what your
character is thinking and doing in as normal a way as you can. You
shouldn't have to spell it out for your audience. So, unless it is
absolutely vital, beware of having characters on their own for any
length of time. Such 'monologues' are hard to write and especially
to keep natural. They so easily become stilted, and being so, lose
all their interest and believability.

You must invent different ways of doing things and different
ways of saying things all the time. This is the fascination of writing, just as much for radio as anything else. Keep your material
fresh.

Once again, you will come up against the problem of economy

of words. This applies just as much to dialogue as it does to any other form of writing. Examine the way you speak. Listen to someone else speaking, and you'll find that every sentence uttered has a rhythm and a flow. This applies to your writing, too. One word too many and the impact you've been striving for will disappear, as does that one vital word too few. If your sentences are too long they become 'woolly', which means wordy, and if they are too short they are 'scrappy'.

If you're not sure whether you're too long or too short, one tip is to read the dialogue aloud to yourself. You'll soon find out. A lot depends on your characters. If your main character is pedantic, then using long words in an intellectual manner is in character, but normally you should aim for colloquial content.

Are your lines easy to say?

Every writer is guilty of producing the occasional line which is 'not easy to say' at some time or other. You've written your play, sketch or sit-com, the producer has read it, and the actors like it. What could be more straightforward than that? Nothing, until you come to the rehearsal, and then, completely out of the blue, your leading actress goes over to the producer, and with him, comes across to you, and says pleasantly 'I'm sorry, but I just can't say this line.'

It is then your immediate duty to come up with another line which means exactly the same thing but which is easier to say. These 'hard to say' lines do crop up. They are lines which the actor trips over; lines which read perfectly well, but which some people are unable to say aloud. The only way out of this *before* it all happens is to read your script out aloud to yourself, and if any line looks even remotely like being difficult to say, then change it. It'll save you a lot of time and trouble later on.

The long speech

The long speech is another hazard; they are generally not the best idea, and in the hands of the wrong actor can become dull and boring. We know that you can quote long speeches made by Lord Olivier, Dame Peggy Ashcroft and Charles Laughton, but there you are talking about three experts who could read out even the telephone directory and make it absorbing. And not all your actors will be up to that standard!

In any case, a long speech means that we are only hearing from the one person, something we discussed earlier. What do the other characters have to say about it all? Their reactions are important and could further the plot and situation.

And it is worth repeating that long speeches usually mean a writer is trying to wrap the plot up too quickly. Don't do this. Keep it well paced. We cannot emphasise this too much.

Although our next piece of advice could relate to any form of writing, it was raised where a student submitted a radio play, and in the circumstances it seems applicable here. It concerns creating authentic background and knowing your facts.

The student had written the play about miners in South Wales, and in particular about two brothers who knew each other's lives intimately. She had them trapped in the local mine, and while they were waiting to be rescued – or so they hoped – filled up the pages with chat between them. This would have worked well, except that she hadn't done her homework on South Wales miners. If she had, she would have known that they are very close to each other, and that very little goes on between families and friends which they don't know about.

As a result, the two brothers were telling each other mundane things that each of them was already bound to know. As they were on the best of terms, there was no conflict to help the situation, and because of this, what should have been a revealing scene became a collection of words strung together to fill up a few pages. Imagine how this scene could have been transformed: the brothers are trapped in a situation where each depended on the other to save him – the play could have been changed from a polite, boring chat-piece to an explosive drama with all the stops pulled out. The enmity of the two brothers would have pushed the story along nicely until the cave-in (which was how the student ended the play) and there wouldn't have been any forced and unnatural dialogue.

So even though in radio you really can please yourselves as to what you write about and where it takes place, make sure you know all the essential details about your background material. In the example above, 'background' meant South Wales mining life, what the people are and how they live. If you don't, your character and plot writing will suffer, your writing will take on a hint of desperation, and you will probably wind up with a rejection slip.

Although so far we have dealt mainly with radio drama you can be sure that anyone submitting material for radio – talks, documentaries, comedy scripts, and so on – will receive much encouragement from all concerned. But don't forget to study your market first. Listen carefully and you will find that Radio 3 and Radio 4 drama is different in content and caters for different types of audience. The market is there for you, but you will have to decide what suits your particular writing talents. If you do this diligently, one of those 600-odd plays the BBC produces every year could well be yours.

The one other large and important aspect of radio we haven't yet touched on is comedy. Radio comedy has always played a big part in the nation's entertainment, and still continues to do so, both with sketch comedy and sit-coms (situation comedy).

Sketch comedy

Again the market is there for you to study. Radio is always on the look-out for new writers, and there are many openings for sketches and bits and pieces in such shows as *The Ken Dodd Show*, *The Grumbleweeds*, Roy Hudd's *The News Huddlines*, and the up-to-the-minute *Week Ending*. New shows often spring up, too, so keep your eyes and ears open for them. Contact the script editors to find out what is being recorded when, so you can send in material in good time.

For the new part-time writer this sort of show is ideal for unsolicited scripts. But the content of each show is tailored to a certain format and style of comedy, so listen to them and study them before you send off your submission. Make sure, for instance, that the sketch you are sending to Ken Dodd is not more suitable for the topical *Week Ending*. Believe us, this is not checked often enough.

Also, check that the show you're sending to actually *wants* unsolicited scripts. If there are only, say, two writers credited the chances are that they don't. The best thing to do is to write to the script editor for information about this and forthcoming shows, and he will give you the details you want.

When writing a comedy sketch, you go for as many laughs, and as quickly, as possible. You will find that sketches are very similar to short stories in their construction and thinking. First you want a strong opening, then a solid middle and a good, strong tag to leave the audience laughing. (A tagline is the final line in your sketch and should also be your last laugh – a big one!) The first laugh should come in your first line if you can manage it; failing that the first line should be the feed to the second, where you get your first laugh. The following gag was done in a sketch some years ago, and raised roars from the audience present, because of a slight innuendo in the second speech:

DOTTIE (ELDERLY LADY. ANNOYED.) Henry! What on earth are you doing? What's keeping you?

RAY (OFF.) Sorry m'dear. I've got me tie caught in me flies!

Naturally, the next line established that Henry was going fishing. No harm done. And just like the short story, you should get on to the theme of your sketch straight away – with laughs.

In any event, sketches are fun to write. The length can be anything up to approximately five minutes cold – that is, without laughs. (You don't need to worry about the length of laughter time, which is difficult to gauge.) However, check on the length required because programmes differ in this.

Sketches are coming back, there is no doubt about that, and perhaps the most popular kind is that below.

Cod sketch

The cod sketch is a send-up of anything or anyone unknown, living, dead, or fictitious!

Naturally, whatever state the subject happens to be in, it should be well-known. If the listeners don't know who or what you are talking about you're on a hiding to nothing.

Let's take two great fictional figures who often appear in this type of sketch, Sherlock Holmes and Doctor Watson. They are perennial favourites, and if you think you can write a sketch about them, go to it. We'll give you an example of the kind of dialogue you could write for them, but don't forget, no matter how seriously they are taken in the drama world, in the world of comedy, Sherlock Holmes is the know-all, a conceited genius of a detective, and Doctor Watson is his dim-wit of a partner, so you get dialogue like this (plus Holmes' unforgettable violin playing, of course):

TAPE (or F/X) SCRAPING VIOLIN PLAYING TUNELESSLY.

WATSON I say, Holmes. Surely your violin would sound better if it had some strings on it – what? (BLUFF LAUGH)

HOLMES I agree Watson. I seem to be playing without

WATSON   rhyme or rosin! Actually, I was thinking about our
next case.

WATSON   Bless me soul, Holmes. Have we drunk the last one
already?

HOLMES   Our next *investigation*, old fellow! Take a look at
this item in the daily paper – *The Nursery News*.

WATSON   Of course, Holmes. (CLEARS THROAT. READS) 'The
Queen of Hearts' – by jove! Royalty in
Hertfordshire! Independence! Whatever next?
(CHUCKLES) Sorry, Holmes. (READS) 'She made some
tarts upon a summer's day. The Knave of Hearts,
he stole those tarts and took them clean away.' I
say! Not cricket, old man. Bounder. Bad form and
all that! Just like young Curvis at college. Took his
girl to a fancy dress ball. She went as a balloon
dancer and he went as a porcupine!

HOLMES   (THOUGHTFUL) He could be innocent, old fellow.

WATSON   No, Holmes! I saw him burst her balloons with my
very eyes!

HOLMES   (TIREDLY) No, Watson, I didn't *mean* Curvis . . .

And so on. As you can see, Watson strays away from the point and
Holmes is brilliant – as usual. The idea behind the sketch was that
Holmes and Watson went back through time to solve a mystery in
Nurseryland, which was novel and original at the time. And the
tag, you ask? Well that was very Holmesian, if there *is* such a
word. The case was solved and Watson again asked the lead question:

WATSON   Well, Holmes, what's next on the agenda?

HOLMES   I don't know what *you* are going to do, Watson old
chap, old fellow, old Doctor, but *I* am going to play
a richly deserved tribute to myself as the greatest
criminal catcher the world has ever known.

WATSON   Bless me soul, Holmes. And what are you going to
play?

HOLMES   A modest little tune, Watson – 'There's No P'lice
Like Holmes!'

It all worked very well, but the tag was a bit of a problem, because
there aren't too many good 'Holmes' tags around.

However, note the 'feel' of the sketch. The dialogue was as the
public anticipates, with a few 'elementarys' spread around in the

script, and the period of the sketch was established in the type of dialogue. In a way, Holmes and Watson have, to the comedy world, become a sort of over-the-top Laurel and Hardy. But in this type of sketch it's still important to get the characters right, even if they *are* cardboard. At least make them sound like the popular concept of a comic Holmes and Watson. It's no use writing them as two comics doing a comic sketch, unless you're writing for personalities instead of comic actors. The above sketch was performed – and brilliantly – by Bob Monkhouse and Kenneth Connor, who played the characters for real, as we imagine someone like Mel Smith and Griff Rhys Jones would. If, on the other hand, it was to be performed by, say, Little and Large, then you would write it for Little and Large, with lots of impressions for Eddie Large. It would be 'personal' sketch writing, which is a different thing altogether; here you write around the personalities of your stars, and exploit their talents as comedians to the full.

If you submitted any material to *The Ken Dodd Show*, then you would write gags about Knotty Ash, The Diddymen, Ken's teeth and so on, all to do with Ken Dodd, and unusable by any other comedian. You would tailor your gags and sketches to your star. Similarly, if you are submitting material for *Week Ending* it should be highly topical and satirical.

Many sketch writers, having decided on the subject for their sketch, sit down with a pencil and some paper and think up a list of gags around that subject before they actually start their sketch. They use key words, and think of as many associations with the subject as they can. This is a process to be recommended as it can save a lot of time, and in many cases will give you several ideas for taglines before you even start.

There are many favourite topics for the cod sketch, which is often referred to as 'The Big Sketch'. Jungle sketches often appeal, in which case you bring it up to date by adding a topical hero like Indiana Jones, who, more often than not, is seen in jungle surroundings. We'll take some key jungle-type words and show you how to make jungle jokes from them.

KUKRI: A knife for cutting through the undergrowth.

Gag: 'It comes with an instruction manual.
What's it called? – *A Kukri Book*!'

Or:

BEARER: One of the men you take on your expedition to carry the supplies. Another link is our five pound note. Gag:

INDIANA	Rule two – when you go into the jungle, always take a supply of five pound notes with you.
MAN	Great Scot, Mr Jones. Why?
INDIANA	When the bearer asks you for money, you give him one. If you haven't noticed, on every five pound note it says 'I promise to pay the bearer on demand.'

Or:

HEAD COOK & BOTTLE WASHER: He cooks heads and washes bottles.

You can see the idea. Make a list of all the thoughts that come into your minds connected with the jungle and go from there.

The same routine applies to other sketches. James Bond's latest film will serve as the subject for an up-to-date sketch. There always seems to be a new science fiction film around these days. Anything from or in Outer Space will give you plenty of material for a big sketch, but don't ever forget! It has to be about something or someone that the public are familiar with, otherwise the only one who sees all the funny lines and knows what they mean is you. You can use the characters' correct names, or make funny variations on them for laughs. Even the weakest looking lines can become laughs in the right context.

Certain subjects and lines will always be with us, such as 'Robin Hood, the man who Maid Marion'; and when one of Robin's men was found in a compromising position with a damsel – 'Was Will Scarlett!'

Ever since the immortal King Kong we've had monster sketches. We've had monster bees, spiders, ants, rats, monsters that have been frozen since the Ice Age and brought back to life by atomic explosions in the North Pole having changed the temperature.

Historical sketches, too, make marvellous vehicles for gags. They never date. You can always bring in modern observation for added laughs. For instance:

| SOLDIER | The Roman Army's landed, sire. They're heading straight for London. |

CAPTAIN   Don't worry. They'll never get through High
          Wycombe - it's murder on a Saturday!

Narrators are always useful in dramatic sketches to heighten
the fun:

NARRATOR   (TENSELY) We engaged the monster winkles on
           Bagshott Common – behind the bus shelter! The
           entire might of Britain was there – the Army, the
           Air Force and the Royal Navy! It took ages to get
           the *Ark Royal* on to the grass!

After the 'big' or 'cod' sketch, there is the 'idea sketch'.

The idea sketch

This is also known as the 'wouldn't-it-be-funny-if' sketch. The
basis of it is to switch or to twist the idea in some way, sometimes
by transposing one thought on top of another. Here are a few
instances of this kind of sketch.

'Keeping up with the Joneses'
The idea came one lunchtime, and didn't start with us. Someone
mentioned the phrase 'keeping up with the Joneses' and immediately it struck a chord – one more illustration of why you should
be looking and listening for ideas at all times. 'Keeping up with
the Joneses' we mused, 'a funny sketch idea.' The next step was to
decide who was keeping up with the Joneses, and about what.
After some deliberation, we thought of divorce. Ideal! The idea of
someone having a divorce and someone else wanting to 'keep up
with them' by having one as well, appealed very much.

But who would be nutty enough to want to do this? They had to
be believable and likable. And so our heroes became the very
elderly Colonel Blakeney, ex-Indian Army, and his dithery wife
Amy. Their next-door neighbours, the Joneses, hadn't beaten
them up to now. The Blakeneys had matched them in everything
they'd done, but needless to say, not this time. They didn't have
their divorce, because when it was explained to them by their
solicitor they decided they loved each other too much. And when
the solicitor asked them why they wanted one in the first place the
tag of 'keeping up with the Joneses' came in. It worked well.

The army takes over

We are always having strikes in this country, but at the back of our minds is the thought that if things really get out of hand, the Army will take over. Comforting.

This idea was the basis of a very funny sketch and it can be switched to suit all sorts of situations. In ours, however, we decided that the BBC would come out on strike. All the technicians, producers, scriptwriters and actors would come out on strike, leaving all those fans of the well-known serial *The Archers* champing at the soundless bit.

But no! The Army moved in, and we had soldier actors and actresses, soldier scriptwriters, army producers – in fact it became an armyfied *Archers*, filling their half-hour with an everyday story of army folk.

For whom the bell tings

The basic idea here was that nothing is more irritating than standing in the cold and the rain waiting for a bus to come along, and finally, three come along at the same time!

People will do anything to avoid queueing for a bus, we reasoned – cadge a lift, walk, go by train, anything. So, what can be done to make them look forward to the arrival of that elusive bus? The answer was to give them entertainment – yes, a cabaret on the bus.

And for the artists themselves, what a proud moment to be top of the bill on the 154 from Sutton in Surrey to Morden Underground Station!

How do you mount a sketch of this kind? Something like this:

TAPE or F/X BUS ENGINE TICKING OVER. THE BELL TINGS. REV. UP
         ENGINE AND LOSE UNDER
CLIPPIE   Good evening passengers, and welcome to . . .
         'Double Decker Dazzle!'
TAPE or F/X APPLAUSE
CLIPPIE   And this is your hostess and clippie, Angela Ripoff
         . . .
DRIVER   . . . and your Driver, Fred Noggin up here in front,
         saying . . .
BOTH   (SING) Good evening friendssssss!
CLIPPIE   Welcome to the 154, the Tops in Entertainment.
         Tonight's lucky ticket wins the first prize of a
         honeymoon trip for two on the Green Line from
         Windsor to Wapping . . .

DRIVER	And the *second* prize is . . . wait for it, wait for it . . .
BOTH	*Two* trips on the Green Line from Windsor to Wapping!
CLIPPIE	But now it's laughter time on the 154. London Regional Transport have pleasure in presenting your own . . . your very own Mister Mirth himself . . . a big welcome please, for . . . (Etc . . . Etc . . .)

'Come with me to the casbah'

This really comes into the 'what-can-we-do-about-old-films' category. Old films are particularly good for those looking for 'idea sketch' material.

What is funny about old films? Well, the fact that some of them have been shown so often over the years that they have broken and been stuck together again . . . and then they've broken again and been stuck together again, ad infinitum.

Obviously, having been broken and stuck together again so many times, the dialogue and the pictures are inclined to jump all over the place, with a crisp crackle every time they do so. As a result, you hear the crackle (CSK) and the picture and dialogue change to a completely different scene. Suddenly, everyone is talking about something else!

In our sketch this background was all made clear in the introduction, and the actors did the crackle personally and verbally. It was great fun for the performers, and equally good fun for the audience, both at home and in the studio. As we have said, the dialogue changed abruptly with the change of scene, and it went like this:

IRMA	Pepe, you shouldn't be here. In the Casbah you are safe, but here in the Market Place, your life is in danger. Every minute, every second means instant – (CSK) – coffee?
PEPE	Black, please. Two lumps. (ROMANTIC) My darling Irma, let me gaze once more upon your eyes, your lips, upon your – (CSK) – two immense hills?
IRMA	I am familiar with them. The jewels lie between them.
PEPE	How I long to get my hands on them. (Etc . . . Etc . . .)

'Two tiddles don't make a wink'

The message here is that violence abounds in sport. Tennis

players throw their racquets at each other after a row, and one day perhaps they'll even throw the umpire!

In soccer and rugby it is just as sickening, although in soccer the two teams do kiss and make up as they leave the field. So, what is funny about violence in sport, and *is* it funny? Yes it is, if you apply it to a sport like – tiddleywinks! And even more so if you make the game between Clotford, the Conservative Champions of southern England, and their age-old rivals, Twitley, the Working Mens' Club Champions of the north.

'The Battle of Waterloo'

Getting on to a train during the rush hour can sometimes be practically impossible, so what do you do about it? You fight your way on, otherwise you don't *get* on! Commuting these days is bad enough, but in a few years' time it could be organised guerilla warfare, with white-collar combat units banding together in a desperate battle for seats. In other words, it's the Battle of Waterloo, all over again!

'Collectors' world'

These days, people are becoming Antique Crazy. They will pay all sorts of exorbitant prices for any article that is reputed to be a relic of a bygone age. All they want to do is to take it home to make their friends and neighbours jealous.

That is today. But what about tomorrow? Will the commonplace possessions of today become the antique collector's joy tomorrow – say in 500 years' time?

'The pavement artists'

Pictures are always interesting, that is, paintings and drawings. But you know what the saying is, that if the artist is deceased his paintings will sell for a fortune. When he's alive, he can starve to death and nobody cares, but the moment he dies, something magical happens to his paintings. Everyone wants them. Is it scarcity value or what?

Whatever it is it can apply to all sorts of artists, including those very clever – and often hard-up – pavement artists, who display their talents on the pavement flagstones:

TAPE or F/X TRAFFIC NOISES. ESTABLISH AND LOSE

CHARLIE   (OLD) 'Ere, Eddie . . . you're very quiet.
EDDIE   (OLD) That's because I'm not saying anything, Charlie. I'm thinking.

CHARLIE What you thinking about then Eddie?

EDDIE (WHEEZING COUGH) Well . . . I'm thinking about R.I.Peeing myself.

CHARLIE R.I. . . . (PAUSE) . . . eh?

EDDIE Exactly. You've caught on. I'm thinking of making me, Eddie – deadie, me, Edward – deadward, me, Ed – dead!

CHARLIE (EMOTIONAL) But you can't do it, Eddie. Think of what you're leaving behind you!

EDDIE (CYNICAL LAUGH) *What?* Just tell me *what*, Charlie! Just you tell me one thing of value what I'm leaving behind . . .

CHARLIE Well, *me*, for a *start*!

EDDIE Yeh! You and a worn-out cap with an Irish penny in it, and I'm not going all the way over there to spend it!

CHARLIE (BROKENLY) Eddie, don't do it old mate. Think of all the 'appy times we've 'ad together . . . life isn't all that bad. Life's worth livin' no matter what. Give up the idea, Eddie . . . Give it up – eh?

EDDIE (CRYING WITH WHEEZING LAUGHTER) Dear oh dear, Charlie. You are dim. Sometimes I think there's even less to you than meets the eye . . .

CHARLIE (BAFFLED PAUSE) Er . . . fanks, Eddie . . .

EDDIE I'm not *really* going to R.I.P. meself in – I'm only going to *pretend* to . . .

And Charlie then catches on as Eddie explains his plan, and the sketch develops.

We hope that by now you have got the idea behind sketch writing. Think funny! Let your imagination run riot. What you have read in this chapter just about covers the main canvas of sketch writing and the ways to think of ideas. Read something, listen to something, see something and think 'Wouldn't it be funny if . . .?'

Situation comedy

As we are going to deal with writing situation comedy in depth in the next chapter, there is not a lot to say about it here. Simply remember that you are writing for radio, and in radio writing words are the medium.

Summing up

1 The radio listener wants to know everything that is happening in words – your words. People can't see what is happening. You must tell them everything.
2 Don't ignore the great aids to your writing in the shapes of music and effects.
3 Get your background right.
4 Listen to radio and do your market research thoroughly.
5 Watch your word economy.
6 Don't leave your characters on their own for lengthy periods to talk to themselves and explain the plot to the listeners.
7 Think original and think funny!

6. Writing for Television

It is true to say that television has now become the major market for the writer, and will continue to be so for the foreseeable future. Just take the present situation and look at the many opportunities open to the writer. There is the BBC, which broadcasts nationally on its two channels, BBC 1 and BBC 2, and in addition to the national network, the BBC also has many regional television stations which have an input to the national network and occasionally produce and transmit their own programmes of local interest. Then there is the Independent Television Network, which, at the time of writing, consists of the Big Five – Thames, London Weekend, Central, Granada and Yorkshire, plus all the other smaller regional companies such as Anglia, TVS, TSW, Border, Harlech, STV, Tyne Tees, Channel, Grampian and Ulster.

In addition, there are Channel 4, Sky TV, British Satellite Broadcasting, Cable TV and Superchannel. A further 5th channel is shortly to be launched and it is only a question of time before this is followed by even more channels. If you also take into consideration the many independent television production companies that are springing up, it is obvious that the outlets for a writer in television are tremendous.

Every television company, some of them now transmitting programmes 24 hours a day, is constantly on the look-out for ideas and scripts to satisfy this gargantuan appetite.

In this chapter we will cover every aspect of television writing, looking at:

1 The one-off play.
2 Series and serials.
3 Situation comedy.
4 Variety programmes.
5 Game shows.
6 Documentaries.

We have already stressed the fact that when you are writing for television it is most important that you think in visual terms, and we make no apology for repeating ourselves. When your script lands on the desk of a television producer the first thing he or she will look for is its visual content. If your script isn't visual it will not get produced, no matter how brilliant your dialogue may be.

Before we proceed to examine the various aspects of television writing, we would like to say a few words about television itself. Your play, situation comedy or whatever you write, will be recorded mainly in a television studio. This imposes certain limitations on the writer of which you should be aware. Most television companies have at least one major studio of between 8000 and 10 000 square feet which they use for both drama and situation comedy. Try and visit a studio if you can. Telephone the department concerned with the particular subject for which you wish to write – drama or light entertainment. Explain that you are planning to write for television and would like to visit the studios. Many television companies organise tours from time to time, one of which you may be able to join. Failing that, apply for tickets to an audience show – a game show, a variety show or a situation comedy.

You will see that in the case of a situation comedy there will be up to five studio sets, depending upon the size of each set, the remainder of the studio space being taken up by the seating for the studio audience. When a drama is recorded in the studio, this seating is dismantled and the entire studio space devoted to the sets: there may be up to ten or twelve sets, again depending on the size of each. You must therefore tailor your play or sitcom to the studio requirements. Remember, the larger each set is, the less room you will have left for the others. So keep your sets a reasonable size – don't ask for the interior of the Guildhall, or the Terminal One departure lounge at Heathrow Airport. Some things are impossible, even for the best set designer.

One final thing to bear in mind is the use of film (OB – outside broadcasts). Whilst a couple of scenes shot on location will help to broaden a television play, you should not overload your play with too much film for two reasons. Firstly, there's the cost factor. Location filming is very expensive. And secondly, most television companies will not want their studios to be idle, while most of your play is being recorded out on location. So keep it in the studio and everybody will be happy.

One more thing before we get down to specifics. If you possibly can, keep your cast of characters as small as you can. Unless a particular character is vital to your storyline and helps to move the plot along, drop the character. Too many characters spoil the plot. Also, you'll be saving on the budget in terms of fees and wardrobe costs.

Before a producer or script editor reads the opening lines of your script he will have looked at the number of studio sets you have listed, the size of the cast and the amount of location filming you have requested. The front page of your script should list these details. So if you want to keep him or her in a receptive frame of mind as he reads on, don't have 24 sets, four days filming and a cast of thousands.

The single play

In recent years there has been a decline in the number of single plays, in favour of the drama series (like *All Creatures Great and Small* and *Minder*), the mini-series such as Dennis Potter's *Blackeyes*, and book adaptations, such as *The Ginger Tree* by Christopher Hampton. This is partly due to rising production costs – it is far more economical to amortise the cost of studio sets over a period of 13 or 26 weeks – and partly due to the belief of some programme makers that the single play no longer appeals to the viewer.

However, television trends have a habit of changing fairly often and it's only a question of time before the single play undergoes a renaissance. At the moment it lives on under the guise of films for television and anthology series, such as *Tales of the Unexpected* and so on.

The first thing you must do as you sit at your table is to go through your synopsis carefully and break it down into scenes so that you know in advance how many studio sets you will require and the amount of filming you need. For example let's take the following synopsis:

DARBY AND JOAN
Darby and Joan are Tommy and Betty Dixon. They are both in their sixties, Tommy is 65 and Betty 61. They live in a semi-detached house typical of many to be found in the outskirts of any large industrial town.

It is Tommy's last day at the engineering factory where he has worked for the last forty years. He is retiring. Both Tommy and Betty are looking forward to his retirement and to spending more time in each other's company, but after spending forty years during which the longest time they ever saw each other was at weekends, they discover that twenty-four hours a day is too much for both of them.

They get off to a bad start. Betty has arranged a little surprise party for Tommy with their next door neighbours, Derek and Jean, but Tommy is taken for a drink after work with his boss and workmates, where he is presented with a clock, drinks too much and arrives home much the worse for wear. Needless to say, Betty is far from pleased. The next morning, Tommy gets a shock when Betty won't get up to cook his breakfast. She wants a bit of retirement too. Things go from bad to worse. Betty and Tommy get on each other's nerves. She wants him to help her with the housework – he doesn't see why he should. They discover that they can barely live on their joint pensions. Tommy tries to get his old job back, but without success. He tries to get a part-time job, but it's the same story – he's too old.

They have an almighty quarrel and Tommy goes off in a temper.

Tommy's ex-boss arrives to tell Betty that if Tommy is interested he needs a gardener two days a week. Just then there is a knock on the door. It's a policeman. He says an old gentleman has just been knocked down by a car and taken to hospital. The only proof of his identity was a pension book. He shows it to Betty. It is Tommy's.

Betty goes to the hospital. She is told to wait. She sits next to a man who turns out to be the car driver. He tells Betty that Tommy just stepped straight out off the pavement. He couldn't avoid him. Upset as she is, Betty tries to comfort him. The man goes and a Sister approaches. Betty is told that Tommy is dead.

Derek and Jean have had a phone call from Betty at the hospital telling them the news, and are getting ready to go and pick Betty up. They hear a noise from next door, and think the house is being burgled. Derek goes to investigate, and finds Tommy! It appears that Tommy was drinking with a friend, ran out of money and borrowed five pounds. As security, he made his friend take his pension book. Tommy goes to the hospital where he meets Betty. That evening they are in the pub, when Tommy's ex-boss comes in. He repeats his offer of a gardening job for Tommy, and says that he also could do with a cleaner, two days a week. Betty could be there on the same days as Tommy. They accept the jobs on condition that they go on different days. The less time they have together, the better.

As you can see, the theme for this play is that of relationships. How to cope with retirement is a problem that faces more and more people today, so there is a lot of audience identification with the idea. It has an interesting beginning, a good middle with plenty of opportunities for conflict and suspense, and a satisfactory ending. If you read the synopsis again, there are certain studio sets which are immediately obvious – the Dixon house, the factory, the next door neighbours' house, the pub and the hospital. The Dixon house would probably be three sets, the kitchen, the lounge and the bedroom; the factory would be two, the boss's office and the factory floor. There is also the hospital waiting room. So that's a total of nine sets, which leaves you enough scope to add one or two more in your scene breakdown. The synopsis also indicates a couple of areas where the use of film would be an advantage. The main characters involved in the play are described too.

Your scene breakdown from such a synopsis should read something like this:

1 *Exterior. Dixon back garden. Film. Day.*
It's afternoon. Betty is putting some bread out for the birds. She sees her neighbour Jean. They chat about various things (rising prices, their health etc). Betty invites Jean in for a cuppa.

2 *Interior. Dixon kitchen. Studio. Day.*
Betty and Jean having a cup of tea. Establish that today is Tommy's big day. He is retiring after a lifetime's work. Reveal that Jean has invited Tommy and Betty to a celebratory dinner with her and her husband Derek. It's going to be a surprise for Tommy – he knows nothing about it.

3 *Interior. Factory. Studio. Day.*
Introduce Tommy. He is being ribbed by his workmates on his impending retirement . . . 'all right for some eh? . . . breakfast in bed will it be? . . . every day a holiday'.

4 *Interior. Jean's lounge. Studio. Day.*
Jean showing Betty a cake she has baked for Tommy. Derek

home from his job at a supermarket. Discuss Tommy. He'll just be knocking off now for the last time.

5 *Interior. Factory. Studio. Day.*
Tommy switching off his lathe. He's a bit sad, despite it all. Also disappointed that the boss hasn't put in an appearance. He'd expected a handshake, if not something more substantial. He mentions going to the pub for a farewell drink, but his workmates fob him off with various excuses, except for one man who agrees to go.

6 *Interior. Pub. Studio. Day.*
Tommy and his friend arrive for a drink. Tommy is grumbling about none of his other workmates caring enough to join them. Suddenly, they all burst in with shouts of 'Surprise'. Tommy realises it had all been a joke.

7 *Interior. Dixon lounge. Studio. Night.*
Betty is getting ready for her evening out.

8 *Interior. Pub. Studio. Night.*
Tommy happily drinking with his mates.

9 *Interior. Dixon lounge. Studio. Night.*
Betty, now slightly worried. Looking at her watch.

10 Interior. Pub. Studio. Night.
Tommy being presented with a clock by the boss. More drinks arriving.

11 *Exterior. Street. OB. Night.*
Betty on the doorstep looking anxiously up and down. Jean emerges from next door. Betty says she can't understand where Tommy could be.

12 *Interior. Pub. Studio. Night.*
Tommy is now very happily inebriated. One of the lads asks Tommy if it isn't time he went home – Betty may be worried about him. Tommy shakes his head. 'No, I'm all right. I've got a very understanding wife!'

13 *Interior. Jean's lounge. Studio. Night.*
Betty furious. 'Wait till he gets home. I'll murder him!' They decide to start dinner without Tommy.

14 *Interior. Pub. Studio. Night.*
Tommy being persuaded to go.

15 *Interior. Jean's lounge. Studio. Night.*
Betty having coffee. They've finished the meal. Derek tries to make excuses for Tommy. After all, he didn't know they were planning this surprise.

16 *Interior. Pub. Studio. Night.*
Nearly closing time. Tommy enters. Barman is surprised to see him. 'I thought you'd gone.' Tommy grins, 'I had. But I left my clock behind!' He goes to get his clock. 'Now I'm back, I'll just have one for the road!'

17 *Exterior. Street. OB. Night.*
Tommy walking unsteadily down the street. He passes a fish and chip shop, stops and goes in.

18 *Interior. Dixon lounge. Studio. Night.*
Betty waiting grimly. She hears the front door open and close. Tommy enters. 'I'm back love.' Betty stares, disgusted. 'I've brought you some chips.' Betty tells him what he can do with them. Tommy is trying to apologise when he remembers he's left his clock in the chip shop.

19 *Interior. Dixon bedroom. Studio. Day.*
The following morning. Tommy awake at his usual time. Betty says now he's retired they can lie in. He says he's hungry. Wants his breakfast. Betty tells him to get it himself.

20 *Interior. Dixon kitchen. Studio. Day.*
Tommy in a bad mood. He's burnt the toast, broken a cup and let the kettle boil dry. Betty comes in. Tommy has plans to sit and read the paper, then watch TV. Betty has other plans for him. The gutters need cleaning out – the outside of the house needs repainting and the drains need looking at.

21 *Montage of scenes.*
Several quick scenes showing Tommy hard at work doing various jobs in and around the house.

22 *Interior. Pub. Studio. Day.*
Lunchtime. Several days later. Tommy telling the barman that he's never worked so hard in his life, since he retired.

23 *Interior. Dixon lounge. Studio. Day.*
Betty and Tommy talking. She tells him that they can't manage on their pensions. Tommy says he will get a part-time job.

24 *Interior. Job centre. Studio. Day.*
Tommy arrives to look for a job. No luck. They have nothing.
He's too old. A young lad tells him they are looking for staff
at a new supermarket.

25 *Interior. Supermarket. OB. Day.*
Tommy asking the manager for a job. No luck again. They
want young people.

26 *Interior. Pub. Studio. Day.*
Tommy asking if they need part-time help, but they don't.

27 *Interior. Factory. Studio. Day.*
Tommy tries to get his old job back, but it's been filled.

28 *Interior. Dixon lounge. Studio. Day.*
Tommy sitting glumly. Betty comes in to say she has had the
offer of a cleaning job. Tommy forbids her to accept it. He
won't have his wife working. He is too proud. They have a
flaming row. Tommy storms out of the house.

29 *Interior. Jean's lounge. Studio. Day.*
Betty telling her troubles to Jean.

30 *Exterior. Park. OB. Day.*
Tommy sitting on a park bench. Sad and depressed. A
woman passes, pushing a pram. She drops her purse.
Tommy picks it up and opens it. It's full of money. For a
moment he's tempted, then he runs after the woman and
hands it to her.

31 *Interior. Dixon lounge. Studio. Day.*
Betty ironing. Tommy's ex-boss calls to say he can give
Tommy a part-time job. Two days a week, doing his garden.
A knock on the door. It is a policeman with the news that
Tommy has been knocked down. He was crossing the road
when a car hit him. They identified him by his pension book
which was in his pocket. He's been taken to the hospital in a
serious condition.

32 *Interior. Hospital corridor. Studio. Day.*
Betty is sitting. She has been told to wait. A young man
arrives and sits next to her. Not knowing who Betty is, he
tells her that he knocked Tommy down. He is in a state of
shock and says that Tommy just stepped out in front of his
car. Betty tries to comfort him. A Sister arrives and tells Betty
to go with her.

33 *Interior. Sister's office. Studio. Day.*
Betty asks how Tommy is, and if she can see him. The Sister
shakes her head. 'I'm sorry, Mrs Dixon. We did all we could.'
Betty realises Tommy is dead.

34 *Interior. Jean's lounge. Studio. Day.*
Jean is waiting for Derek. She had a phone call from Betty
telling her the bad news, and she in turn called Derek. Derek
arrives to take Jean to the hospital. As they are about to go,
they hear a noise from next door. Derek decides to
investigate.

35 *Interior. Dixon lounge. Studio. Day.*
Derek has let himself in with the spare key. To his
amazement, Tommy emerges from the kitchen. Derek tells
him that they all thought he was dead. Tommy reveals that
he went in the pub, and borrowed five pounds from an old
friend, and as security, made the old friend take his pension
book. It is obviously the friend who was knocked down.

36 *Interior. Sister's office. Studio. Day.*
Betty is being comforted by the sister. They are waiting for
the body to be brought from the operating theatre. Betty has
insisted on seeing him. The sister gets a phone call. The
body is now in a private room. She gives Betty instructions.

37 *Interior. Hospital corridor. Studio. Day.*
Tommy enters. He sees Betty walking away from him, and
calls. They are re-united.

38 *Interior. Pub. Studio. Night.*
Tommy, Betty, Derek and Jean celebrating Tommy's return
from the dead. His ex-boss enters and repeats his offer of a
job for Tommy, adding that Betty could also do two days a
week housework. They accept on condition that they work
on different days. For Tommy and Betty, absence makes
their hearts grow fonder!

If you study the scene breakdown, you will see that you now
have a very good base from which to start writing the script. Each
scene follows on logically from the one before, and the action
flows smoothly from scene to scene. Before you start to write you
also know the content of each scene and this will enable you to
write the dialogue much more easily. If this scene breakdown was
for a play to be produced by Independent Television you would

need to indicate where you wish the commercial breaks to take place. In this case, assuming that the play will run for one hour, your commercial breaks could follow the end of scenes 13 and 28. If you look at these scenes you will find that they both end at a point which leaves the viewers wondering what happens next. A 'cliffhanger'.

Many inexperienced writers have difficulty in judging the length of their finished script and a question we are often asked is 'How many pages should I write?' Well, of course it depends on several things – how much action is in the play as opposed to dialogue, and whether it is a slow, moody piece or fast-moving and pacey. As a general rule, we have found from experience that if you allow half a minute for each page you won't be far out.

And remember, when you have written your play have it typed before you submit it. The front page should contain the title of the play and who it is written by. The next page should contain the title again, then the cast list, the number of studio sets, and the scenes which you require to be filmed on location.

When you actually start to write the dialogue it is important to describe the various sets as you see them. Does the Dixon lounge contain modern or old-fashioned furniture; is there a door; where does it lead to; is there a window; can it be opened; are there any pictures on the walls; what ornaments are in the room? All this you must decide in your own mind before you start to write. If you have a clear picture of the room it will help you to write visually. A room and its contents also tells the viewer a lot about the people who live there and their social standing.

Similarly, with your characters. Describe how you see them, their age, and how they are dressed. And most important, when they speak, describe their attitudes and emotions. This will give the director and actor an indication of how you wish a line to be spoken. There is a wealth of difference between **A**:

WIFE   Mother phoned darling. She's coming to stay with
            us for a month. Won't that be nice?
HUSBAND   (ENTHUSIASTIC) Wonderful.

and **B**:

WIFE   Mother phoned darling. She's coming to stay with
            us for a month. Won't that be nice?
HUSBAND   (GLUMLY) Wonderful!

Just by the use of one word, it is clear that the attitude of husband

B is totally different from that of husband A. So it is extremely important that you ask yourself, as you are writing the script 'What is my character thinking as he speaks a line?' This is not to say that every single line of dialogue must have a stage direction, only those where it is necessary to convey a mood or attitude which can affect the meaning of a particular line. Also, still keeping that visual image in the forefront of your mind, you should describe what your various characters are doing. Are they sitting down, standing up, reading a paper, having a drink? Describe every piece of action in detail. For example:

INTERIOR BAKER BEDROOM. DAY.
A LARGE MODERN BEDROOM, WITH FITTED FURNITURE. THERE IS A BAY
WINDOW WITH THE CURTAINS STILL DRAWN. A DOOR LEADS TO AN EN-
SUITE BATHROOM. A COUPLE OF CONTEMPORARY PRINTS ADORN THE
WALLS. A SHAPELESS MOUND IS UNDERNEATH THE BEDCLOTHES ON THE
KING-SIZED BED. JANE EMERGES FROM THE BATHROOM. SHE IS IN HER
EARLY THIRTIES. SHE IS WEARING A DRESSING GOWN AND HAS A TOWEL
WRAPPED ROUND HER HEAD LIKE A TURBAN. SHE MOVES TO THE BED AND
ADDRESSES THE MOUND.

JANE   Matt! (THERE IS A GRUNT FROM UNDER THE BEDCLOTHES)
        Matthew!! (ANOTHER GRUNT. JANE PULLS THE BEDCLOTHES
        DOWN TO REVEAL MATT'S FACE. HIS EYES ARE CLOSED) Are
        you asleep?

MATT   Yes!

JANE   It's eight o'clock.

MATT OPENS HIS EYES AND GROANS.

MATT   (BLEARILY) What year is it?

JANE   How do you feel?

MATT   How do I look?

JANE   Terrible.

MATT   (SORRY FOR HIMSELF) That's how I feel!

JANE CROSSES TO A DRESSING TABLE UNIT.

JANE   (SITTING DOWN) Don't expect any sympathy from me.

MATT   (SITTING UP AND GROANING) I think that veal I had last
        night was off. (CLUTCHING HIS MIDDLE) It's upset my
        stomach.

JANE   (CROSSLY) It wasn't the veal that upset your stomach. It
        was the two litres of red wine, it was floating about in!
        (SHARPLY) Come on – get out of that bed.

(MATT SLOWLY SWINGS HIS LEGS OFF THE BED, THEN PUSHES HIMSELF UP
UNTIL HE IS STANDING. HE SWAYS A LITTLE, THEN STARTS TO WALK
TOWARD THE BATHROOM. AT THE DOOR HE STOPS AND GROANS AGAIN.

MATT
JANE   (SIMULTANEOUSLY) Never again.

MATT STARES AT JANE, PULLS HIS TONGUE AT HER AND DISAPPEARS INTO
THE BATHROOM.

You see how every move is described. You cannot just leave
your characters standing or sitting around. It is rare for any person to be still for any length of time. We are always doing something – a shrug, a gesture, moving from one part of the room to
another. So as well as creating clever and lively dialogue, move
your characters about. Think of something visual they could be
doing during a scene. If you have a scene, for instance, in which a
husband and wife are discussing their children, let them do it
while she is preparing a meal and he is opening a bottle of wine. It
will make the play much more interesting.

Series and serials

A television series is a series of programmes using the same basic
theme and with the same continuing characters, each episode
being self-contained, such as *Bergerac* or *London's Burning*.

A television serial, or 'soap' as they are now called, is a series of
programmes transmitted either daily, as in the case of *Neighbours*,
or three times a week, as with *Coronation Street*, using the same
basic theme and the same characters, but with each episode ending in a 'cliffhanger' so that the viewer will be encouraged to
watch the next one.

Although writing for a series or a serial is usually by invitation
only, some producers are willing to read unsolicited submissions,
especially those concerned with long-running programmes. The
basic techniques for series and serials are the same as those for
any other form of television writing. Keep it visual, have a good
storyline, etc. But the main difference is that you will be writing
for characters which have already been established, who will have
set attitudes already laid down for them. So it is essential that
should you wish to write for a particular series or 'soap', you must
study the series carefully. Watch several episodes, so that you are
aware of the various characters and the way they are played, their
attitudes to one another, their idiosyncracies and what makes
them tick. You must also make sure that the story idea you come
up with fits in to the general pattern of the series or serial, so that
your submission doesn't deviate from the already established format. Many serials have storyline writers, so that the various script

writers involved are given a storyline, with a scene breakdown, which they have to follow. This means that the writer must be disciplined enough to be able to write to a framework, not always easy for a creative person. However, within that framework, as long as the writer covers the various plot points in the storyline, he or she has the freedom to write inventive dialogue – it's not just scripts by committee. It's creative, enjoyable and you get well paid for it.

Situation comedy

Situation comedy is arguably the most difficult form of writing, but it is also the most rewarding, both financially and in terms of personal pleasure. There are very few moments as satisfying as that of hearing a studio audience break into gales of laughter at something which you have written. Most situation comedies are 30 minutes in duration on the BBC and 24½ minutes on ITV, and are transmitted in runs of from seven to thirteen weeks. The theme and the main characters remain the same from week to week, as in *Only Fools and Horses* and *Never the Twain*.

There are several ways in which you can think of a suitable idea for a situation comedy series. One is to look for an occupation or a business within which to set the action which will provide you with enough areas of comedy to sustain several series. Ronnie Wolfe and Ronald Chesney did this very successfully when they wrote *The Rag Trade*, which was set in a clothing factory, and again later in *On the Buses*, set in a bus depot. Another Ronnie, the comedy actor Ronnie Barker set the series *Open all Hours* in a corner shop. However, it is not just enough to think of a good setting. The basis of any successful situation comedy relies on character relationships and the interaction between the characters. In *On the Buses* not every episode was about the actual running of the bus depot – there are only so many stories you can do about that. The humour sprang from the relationship between the Inspector, played by Stephen Lewis, and the bus crew – Reg Varney and Bob Grant. The crew were always trying to put one over on the Inspector, and he was forever trying to catch them out. The writers realised that even this strand of comedy might wear a little thin after a while, so they very cleverly introduced a bit of domestic comedy, in the shape of Reg Varney's home life. Reg lived with his mother, sister and brother-in-law, which gave Wolfe and Chesney many more opportunities for laughs. So when you set out to think of an idea for a situation comedy, make sure your situation has enough scope to sustain the comedy. Most of the obvious situations have already been done – a pub (*Cheers*), a department store (*Are You Being Served?*), a hospital (*Only When I Laugh*), a prison (*Porridge*) and so on, but there are others which could help to spark off an idea.

Another way to find a situation comedy idea is to think of a comedian or comedy actor and devise a vehicle suitable for that person's talents. This method does present certain difficulties, though. Having decided on a particular actor or actress for whom you would like to write, your idea and subsequent script must be carefully tailored to the actor or actress concerned. It wouldn't be any use, for instance, taking Jim Davidson and expecting him to play the part of a county-type Oxbridge graduate who rides to hounds and speaks with a plum in his mouth. Similarly it would be a waste of time to devise a situation comedy for Penelope Keith in which she plays the part of a blowsy cockney barmaid.

In our opinion the best method for creating a successful idea for a situation comedy is to take a situation rather than an occupation, and to create your own characters rather than write for an established 'star' name. This is far more artistically satisfying for the writer. The whole concept is then your own creation; the characters exist because of you, with attitudes created by you. Some examples of series which were devised by using this method are: *Just Good Friends*, written by John Sullivan, which was about two ex-lovers and their renewed relationship when they met again; *For the Love of Ada* written by Vince Powell and Harry Driver, about a gentle love affair between two pensioners, and the opposition they encountered from their respective children; *Last of the Summer Wine*, written by Roy Clarke, which looked at the relationships between three dissimilar men brought together by trying to cope with the boredom of retirement. There are many more: *Love thy Neighbour, Steptoe, Spring and Autumn, Home to Roost*. You will notice that they are all concerned with relationships, the bedrock upon which all successful situation comedies are founded.

It is probably true to say that the most common form of situation comedy, and in many cases the most popular, is the domestic comedy, set in the home, mainly within four walls. This is because the viewers can identify with the situations and can find an echo of themselves and their families within the characters on the screen – the carping mother-in-law, the rebellious son or daughter, the complaining grannie, the boring uncle and so on. Again, domestic comedies are all about relationships, attitudes and emotions, which occur in every family. Knock on any door and you'll find a domestic comedy. And although there have been many domestic comedies in the past there is still a rich seam waiting to be dug. Look at the success of *Bread*. What is it about? Just a Liverpool family, their problems, relationships and attitudes to life. But if you decide to go along this path, your family must have a definite angle. There must be something which makes them stand out, which makes them so interesting that the viewers want to know more about them. In *Bread* it's a family trying to come to terms with life in the north of England, poverty and unemployment. In *Bless This House* it was the generation gap between parents and their children in a rapidly changing world.

There are three other areas of situation comedy which, although limited, deserve to be mentioned. There is the historical situation comedy; the most successful ones which spring to mind are the series of comedies devised and written by David Croft and Jimmy Perry. *Dad's Army*, *Hi-de-Hi* and *'Allo 'Allo* are all taken from situations that occurred some fifty years ago. And of course there is Rowan Atkinson's *Blackadder*. If you are contemplating using an idea taken from the past, one of the most important things you must do is to research the particular era thoroughly so that your facts are historically correct. We should point out that, in spite of the success of the above-mentioned historical situation comedies, some television companies are reluctant to produce them. They are much more expensive to produce than the more normal situation comedy in terms of wardrobe and studio sets, to say nothing of the cost of trying to reproduce the right locations, both geographically and architecturally for any outside filming. The second possible theme is the science fiction situation comedy, such as *Red Dwarf*. But despite having become a 'cult' programme, this only appeals to a minority audience; it has done extremely well on BBC 2, where it has an audience of 4½ million viewers, but if it were on BBC 1, it wouldn't even appear in the top thirty shows. Similarly, with the third area of comedy – fantasy. The Americans have been fairly successful in the past with comedies based on fantasy, such as *Bewitched* and *The Munsters*, but in this country, outside children's programmes, these ideas don't seem to work. Perhaps it's because there's no sense of identification for the viewer, who knows? Having said all that, it's quite possible that a situation comedy series based on science fiction or fantasy will emerge and be a huge success, both critically and commercially. That, as they say, is show business!

Well, we've now looked at the various broad areas that could provide you with an idea on which to base a situation comedy, but what about the writing side. How do you sit down and write a successful sitcom? We're sure it won't come as a surprise to you when we say that the first thing you need is a sense of humour. To be a comedy writer you must be able to see the funny side of life (or even death). And not only that – your sense of humour should be one that will appeal to other people. It's no use writing something that only *you* think is funny. It just wouldn't get accepted. Writing comedy is funny business, if you'll pardon the pun. Nobody can teach you how to write a comedy script. It's a talent you either have or haven't. What we *can* do, however, is to tell you what *not* to do and what mistakes to avoid if you want your script to be favourably received.

The most common mistake that inexperienced writers make when starting to write a situation comedy script is to equate comedy with jokes. But situation comedy is not about jokes. Jokes are what comedians tell in variety shows, whereas the humour in a sitcom should spring naturally from the situation. The secret is to devise a situation in which very ordinary lines become funny. We'll give you a perfect example. You will agree that the words 'Merry Christmas' are not particularly funny, and said in normal circumstances would not even raise a smile. But said by the late Harry Worth in one of his television shows they got a huge laugh from the studio audience, purely because of the situation Harry was in when they were said. It was Christmas Eve. Harry was on his way home from his Auntie's and was waiting on a railway platform for the last train. While he is waiting, a policeman enters.

POLICEMAN	(WITH EXAGGERATED POLITENESS) Good evening, Sir.
HARRY	Ah, good evening, Constable. If you're waiting for the 11.45 it's due any minute.
POLICEMAN	And if *you're* waiting for the 11.45 it's gone!
HARRY	(PUZZLED) Pardon?
POLICEMAN	(GLANCING AT HIS WATCH) It's 11.55.
HARRY	(CHECKING HIS WATCH) Oh dear. My watch must be slow. What time's the next train?
POLICEMAN	Boxing Day.
HARRY	(ALARMED) I can't wait here till then. I've left my

	Christmas pudding on the hob on a low light.
POLICEMAN	(JOKING) It should be well done by the time you eat it then.
HARRY	I don't suppose you could run me home in your car.
POLICEMAN	I'm not in a car. I'm on a bike.
HARRY	Well could you give me a lift on your crossbar?
POLICEMAN	(POINTING TO A PUBLIC TELEPHONE) There's a telephone there. Ring for a taxi.
HARRY	That's a good idea. I'll ring Fred. Do you know his number?
POLICEMAN	(IRRITABLY) How the . . . how should I know his number?
HARRY	Temper, temper – remember it's the season of goodwill.
POLICEMAN	(CONTAINING HIMSELF) Just phone Directory Enquiries.
HARRY	That might be a problem.
POLICEMAN	(EXASPERATED) How can that be a problem?
HARRY	(MILDLY) You're shouting again.
POLICEMAN	I'm sorry. Look – all you have to do is ring Directories, and ask them to give you Fred's number.
HARRY	How will they know which Fred it is?
POLICEMAN	They will when you give them his last name.
HARRY	(SHRUGGING) I told you there'd be a problem. I don't *know* his last name. Are you sure you can't give me a lift on your crossbar?
POLICEMAN	(CROSSLY) No I couldn't.
HARRY	I'll give you a mince pie when we get home.
POLICEMAN	(SHOUTING) I don't want a mince pie. I hate mince pies. And I've got better things to do than to stand here talking to you. It's turned midnight.
HARRY	Has it really?
POLICEMAN	Yes. And I've got a wife and family to get back home to. (TERSELY) Good night.

THE POLICEMAN STARTS TO MOVE OFF

HARRY	Just a moment constable.

THE POLICEMAN STOPS AND TURNS

POLICEMAN	(BAD TEMPERED) Now what do you want?
HARRY	Merry Christmas!

The laugh that followed was because of the innocence of Harry's words and the reaction of the policeman, and came from the situation itself. This is the sort of humour that you should aim for. If you write jokes into your script they will stick out like a sore thumb, unless there is a logical reason for them, such as two of your characters telling jokes in a pub. If you create the right funny situation you will find that the humour will spring out of it naturally. Look for subjects that your characters can talk about with humour. If you're writing a domestic comedy, the attitudes of parents toward pop music, sexual freedom and teenage fashions can provide you with a source of humour which can be funny and believable. You just have to keep on looking for the right situation – that's why it's called *situation* comedy.

But whichever form of situation comedy you choose to write you must always make sure that the situation is believable. Just because it's comedy doesn't mean you have to be unreal. The more truthful the situation, the more believable your characters, the more successful your comedy will be. If you are writing a scene in a solicitor's office, then the solicitor should talk and act like a real solicitor. Exaggeration and 'over the top' performances may be all right for sketch shows but they have no place in a sitcom. And having mentioned sketch shows, let's turn our attention now to that very subject.

Variety programmes

Variety programmes are a good thing for the budding comedy writer to become involved with. Producers of these kinds of programmes, such as *The Russ Abbott Show*, *Hale and Pace* and *Little and Large* are always on the look-out for new and original sketches and quickies. Writing a funny sketch is rather like writing an elongated joke. A sketch can be as short as three minutes or as long as eight, the main criterion being that it must be funny. It must have a funny premise, funny lines and a funny finish, and unlike situation comedy, a sketch can be as unreal as you wish to make it – in fact, the more outrageous and over the top a sketch is, the funnier it is likely to be. When looking for suitable ideas for a sketch, we recommend that you turn to history, novels, films, theatre and television. These will provide you with hundreds of subjects upon which you can base a comedy sketch: the Garden of Eden, primitive man, evolution, the Battle of Hastings, Henry VIII and his wives, the French Revolution, the Wild West, prohibition, Superman, aliens, James Bond, *Brief Encounter*, *EastEnders*, *Neighbours* – the list is endless. But before you actually get down to the writing, think about for whom you are writing the sketch. If you're going to submit a sketch for *The Russ Abbott Show* it can be fairly broad humour, vulgar perhaps but not crude, whereas if you're thinking of writing something for *Hale and Pace* it should be a little more daring and avant garde to suit their style of humour. To give you an example of how to take a subject and turn it into a comedy sketch, we have chosen Noel Coward's *Brief Encounter* and rewritten it for Frankie Howerd.

FRANK	Ladies and Gentlemen. Tonight I am going to give you a little playlet, written by myself, Francis Somerset Howerd, entitled *Brief Encounter*. Yes I know what you're thinking, but you're wrong. *He* knocked it off from *me*. Plagiarism it's called, and he's a proper little plager. He's done it before. He nicked my play about a poultry farm, *This Happy Brood* not to mention my saga of Selfridges *In Which We Serve*. Oh yes he's always at it. However, I digress. On with the playlet. It's a moving sensitive love story about a married man having a bit of the other with someone else's wife – and before you get any funny ideas, I'm not playing the wife. The scene takes place in a railway refreshment room.

INTERIOR. RAILWAY REFRESHMENT ROOM. DAY.

THERE ARE THREE TABLES AND SEVERAL HARD-BACKED CHAIRS. A DOOR
LEADS TO THE PLATFORM. THERE IS A MARBLE-TOPPED COUNTER AND THE
USUAL BUFFET PARAPHERNALIA - SANDWICHES, SCONES AND MEAT PIES
PRESERVED UNDER GLASS. THE ROOM IS EMPTY EXCEPT FOR MYRTLE, A
PLAIN, IF NOT TO SAY UGLY, WAITRESS. SHE IS WEARING CURLERS UNDER
A HEADSCARF AND A TEA-STAINED WHITE OVERALL COAT. FRANK ENTERS.

FRANK	(TO MYRTLE) Excuse me dear, have you got the time?
MYRTLE	Not now ducky, but I'll be off a bit later.
FRANK	If you ask me, you've been off for years.
FRANK	And now we come to the nude seduction scene.

LAURA ENTERS.

LAURA	Just a minute. There's nothing about a nude scene in my script.

FRANK	No, well, I only wrote it in a few minutes ago.
LAURA	Well you can just write it out again.
FRANK	Don't be so prudish. It's all the go now, you know – the nudity bit. They're all at it.
LAURA	Well *I'm* not at it.

LAURA EXITS.

MYRTLE	I'll do it with you.
FRANK	I'm not surprised. From what I've heard you'll do it with anybody! Now let's proceed with the play. *Brief Encounter*. Act two. Several months later.
MYRTLE	(SHOUTING) Tea and sandwiches for the train. Lovely hot pies.
FRANK	We've cut all that dear. We're over-running.
MYRTLE	(ANNOYED) Very nice. For all I've had to say, I might as well not be in this tatty play.
FRANK	Please yourself.
MYRTLE	(TAKING OFF HER OVERALL COAT) Right – I'm going.

MYRTLE EXITS.

FRANK	I knew we'd have trouble with her. They're all the same – these National Theatre Players. (CALLING) Ready when you are Laura.

LAURA ENTERS. HER APPEARANCE SUGGESTS THAT SHE IS EIGHT MONTHS PREGNANT.

LAURA	Darling – there's something I have to tell you.
FRANK	(EYEING HER BULGE) You've left it a bit late dear.
LAURA	Something's come up.
FRANK	I can see that. (TO AUDIENCE) We're getting them all in tonight.
LAURA	My husband is becoming suspicious.
FRANK	I'm not surprised.
LAURA	That's why I'm wearing this disguise.

SHE OPENS HER COAT AND TAKES OUT A CUSHION WHICH SHE HAD STUFFED UNDERNEATH IT.

FRANK	(RELIEVED) Thank God for that.
LAURA	I'd love a cup of tea.
FRANK	(MOVING ROUND THE COUNTER) I'll get you one. Go and sit down.

AS LAURA TURNS A THICK-SET MAN ENTERS. LAURA GASPS

LAURA	My husband.

FRANK DISAPPEARS UNDERNEATH THE COUNTER.

HUSBAND	So this is where you meet your lover. Where is he? I'll murder him.

LAURA	You're mistaken darling. I haven't got a lover.
HUSBAND	Oh yes you have.
LAURA	Oh no I haven't,
HUSBAND	Oh yes you have.
FRANK	(OUT OF VIEW) Oh no she hasn't.
HUSBAND	Who was that?
LAURA	It's the tea lady.

FRANK RISES. HE HAS PUT ON THE OVERALL COAT, AND HAS A TEA TOWEL ROUND HIS HEAD LIKE A SCARF.

FRANK	(IN A FALSETTO VOICE) Good morning. What can I do you for?
HUSBAND	A cup of tea.
FRANK	One tea coming up.
HUSBAND	(AGGRESSIVELY) If I ever catch that wife stealer, I'll beat his brains out.

HE THUMPS THE COUNTER WITH HIS FIST. FRANK SHUDDERS.

FRANK	(PUSHING A CUP OF TEA AT HIM) One tea. Seventy five pee.
HUSBAND	This is diabolical.
FRANK	Not another one complaining. You said you liked the play when you read it.
HUSBAND	I'm talking about the tea.
FRANK	Yes well it *is* a bit stewed. Would you rather have a hot chocolate?
LAURA	Can we please get on with the play?
FRANK	Yes – yes. All right. (TO HUSBAND) Carry on mush.
HUSBAND	(TO LAURA) Laura. Our train leaves in a few minutes. I shall go and wait on the platform. You must decide your own future, but before you do, remember, you have a home waiting for you – a husband who adores you and two lovely children who love you. Are you going to throw all that away, merely for the passing pleasures of the flesh.
FRANK	(IN ADMIRATION) Well done. Two pounds fifty well spent.

THE HUSBAND EXITS. FRANK TAKES OFF THE TEA TOWEL AND COMES OUT FROM BEHIND THE COUNTER.

FRANK	Well darling.
LAURA	I don't know what to do.
FRANK	I love you darling.
LAURA	I love you too darling.

FRANK   You must choose.
LAURA   I can't leave the children
FRANK   I understand.
LAURA   I knew you would.
FRANK   I'll never forget you.
LAURA   Goodbye darling.
FRANK   Goodbye darling.

LAURA EXITS. WE HEAR HER FOOTSTEPS FADE AWAY. THE WHISTLE OF A
GUARD AND A TRAIN PULLING OUT.

FRANK   (HEARTBROKEN) She's gone – gone – gone – gone.
           She's gone.

WE HEAR FOOTSTEPS APPROACHING. FRANK'S FACE LIGHTS UP.

FRANK   She's coming back. She's chosen me. Oh happy
           day. (CALLING) Come to me darling – throw
           yourself into my arms and say you'll never leave
           me.

MYRTLE ENTERS AND THROWS HERSELF INTO HIS ARMS,

MYRTLE   I'll never leave you – you lovely thing.
FRANK   (STRUGGLING) Help – get off me you old ratbag.
FADE OUT.

If you read the sketch carefully, you will see how we have taken
the basic premise of *Brief Encounter* and turned it into a broad comedy. The fact that the viewers may well be familiar with the original film version makes it all the more funny. You will also see that
we have written it in Frankie Howerd's style, although the sketch
itself could be performed by any competent comedian, with the
odd character line changed to fit in with his particular style of
delivery.

The only other form of comedy writing called for in variety
shows is gag writing – writing jokes for certain comedians, such as
Des O'Connor, Jimmy Tarbuck, Marti Caine and so on, but as we
have already covered gag writing in the earlier chapter on writing
comedy for radio, there is little we can add except to stress that
today's style of humour calls for the more sophisticated and topical kind of joke – 'mothers-in-law' are definitely *passé*.

Game shows

There are, and will continue to be in the foreseeable future, many
game shows hosted by well-known celebrities. At the time of
writing there is *You Bet* with Bruce Forsyth, *Blankety Blank* with Les
Dawson, *Telly Addicts* with Noel Edmonds, *Bob's Full House* with

Bob Monkhouse and several others. In addition to this type of programme, there are what we call 'entertainment shows' such as *Surprise Surprise* and *That's Life*. All these programmes require the services of a writer to provide funny introductions, humorous linking material and occasional witty one-liners. Writing for these types of programmes is usually by invitation and submissions are rarely, if ever, accepted. However, if by chance you do become involved in a programme of this nature, you will find it a great help to refer to a *Dictionary of Humorous Quotations*. Another useful source for the snappy one-liner is a dictionary of proverbs. Many of these can be turned into a funny line. For example, take the proverb 'Life begins at forty'. With a little thought that could be changed to 'If life begins at forty, what is it that ends at thirty-nine?' Or how about 'A fool and his money are soon parted'? That could give you 'They say a fool and his money are soon parted – what I want to know is, how did they ever get together in the first place?' It all comes down to what we said earlier, comedy writing requires a keen sense of humour and the ability to see the funny side of everything.

Documentaries

There is not a lot we can say to you about this field, for a documentary is not something you can just sit down and write. Documentaries involve a specialised knowledge of the subject and are not programmes for which you can submit a script, unless you yourself happen to be a specialist in a certain subject or have an unusual hobby which you feel may interest a programme maker. The same applies to another form of writing which is on the increase – scripts used for the corporate video market. Many large companies today use videos to make training films for their staff, and informative technical films to show to prospective clients. Like the documentary, it is a very specialised type of writing and not something that the inexperienced writer should attempt.

Summing up

To summarise briefly this chapter on writing for television:
1 Find out about the medium. Visit a studio.
2 Keep studio sets, cast and filming to a minimum.
3 Break your synopsis down into a scene by scene outline.
4 Think visually at all times.

5 Watch television programmes, particularly those for which you are interested in writing.
6 Write about what you know, or at least, make sure you know something about what you write.

Having given you some inkling of how to write for the small screen, let's turn to a much bigger screen – the cinema – and also to the oldest form of written entertainment for the audience, the theatre.

7. Writing for the Cinema and the Theatre

The cinema

It is difficult for even the most experienced television writer to write a successful screenplay at the first attempt. Conditioned as he or she has been to the requirements and conventions of the small screen, and to writing economically, it takes a while to realise that writing for the big screen really means writing big in every sense of the word. Everything is so much larger – you have to think big – your idea has to *be* big. In the movie business there is rarely, if ever, a restriction on how much of a film is shot on location, and in fact, most movies these days are shot entirely on location, even the interiors. Film budgets are so much larger than those for television and there are fewer constraints on the writer in terms of cast and locations. So when you sit down and try to think of a suitable idea for a film, think big. If you feel that your idea will benefit from having a scene shot say in Paris or Rome or Venice, don't be afraid to put it in. Film producers love exotic and interesting locations. Don't forget, a film has to be good enough to make people get up from their easy chairs, switch off the television and go out to a cinema. So the bigger, the better.

As far as finding a suitable idea for a film the procedure is pretty much the same as we described in our chapter on 'idea awareness'. Films are made about so many varied subjects these days. Just look at the recent best money-making movies at the time we are writing: *Indiana Jones* (adventure); *Batman* (fantasy/adventure); *Ghostbusters* (supernatural); *When Harry Met Sally* (romance); *Lethal Weapon* (cops and robbers); *Back to the Future II* (science fiction). All big block-busting movies, you will note, and that top end of the film industry is very difficult for even experienced scriptwriters to break into; for the inexperienced beginner it's virtually impossible.

Fortunately, there are several independent production

companies springing up who are looking for scripts to make low budget movies, or movies made for television. This market bridges the gap between the small and big screen most admirably, and it is a market that is open to all writers, experienced or not. You will still have to think bigger than Studio One at Shepherd's Bush but not as big as Warner Brothers in Hollywood. A good example of a low-budget movie was *Chariots of Fire*, a film made in Britain and based on a true story of two British Olympic runners. It was produced by David Puttnam and written by Colin Welland. By Hollywood standards the budget was tiny, but in 1981 the film won the Academy Award for Best Picture. It's the old, old story. Money doesn't always buy success. Another low-budget movie that became a huge money-making success was *Crocodile Dundee* starring Paul Hogan. Paul co-wrote the screenplay, and after trying unsuccessfully to raise the money from the big American studios, decided he'd find the cash himself. The finished movie cost around nine million pounds, and when it was released in the US it grossed over seventeen million the first week. That's an example to all of us not to be discouraged.

The main difference between developing an idea for a film as opposed to a television play is that a film company will require a very detailed synopsis and scene breakdown. Some screen synopses run to thirty pages or more. And you must make even more use of visual effects. Your finished screenplay should be such that it could not be made by a television company – it should have the breadth and dimension required for the big screen. One thing to bear in mind when searching for the right idea is to think in terms of international appeal. Sadly, the heyday of the British film industry has long since passed. Gone are those days when films like *The Lavender Hill Mob*, *I'm All Right Jack*, *The Wicked Lady*, *Whisky Galore* and so on poured out of Twickenham, Shepperton, Ealing and Pinewood film studios. Those sort of films would today be considered too parochial, and film companies are looking for ideas that will appeal internationally.

Another market which used to exist for film writers and has now withered away was the television spin-off. Several years ago, feature films were made of successful television shows such as *On The Buses*, *Love Thy Neighbour*, *Dad's Army* and *Bless This House*. They were all low budget films made to cash in on the popularity of the television programmes from which they sprang, and they provided writers with the opportunity for learning the techniques of writing for the cinema.

But back to more practical matters. Suppose you have found an idea which fulfils all the necessary requirements for a movie – a strong storyline with international appeal, a beginning, middle and end, and you've constructed a comprehensive and detailed scene-by-scene breakdown. The actual writing of the screenplay itself will not be so very different from writing a television play. Your dialogue must be sharp – there should be no extraneous scenes, each scene must develop your story a little further, and it should have a large amount of visual content. These rules apply whether you are writing a dramatic film, a love story, a comedy or whatever. It's worth remembering that when the film industry was born, films were silent. There was no dialogue, just a few words now and again on a caption. Writers had no option but to think visually, and it's not a bad idea, when writing a screenplay today, to try and put yourself in that position. Imagine it's a silent movie. See just how much of your story you can get across in visual terms. It's an excellent way to concentrate your thinking, and you will be amazed at how many visual ideas come to you as a result.

We should perhaps warn you that although writing for the cinema, if you are successful, is extremely rewarding in financial terms, it is one of the hardest forms of writing in which to achieve success. Some screenplays are written and re-written over and over again by many different writers, and even then never see the light of day. But on the other hand, you could make it. Think of Colin Welland.

Writing for the theatre

The smell of the greasepaint – the roar of the crowd! There's something magical about the theatre. Of all the forms of writing with which we have been involved, the theatre has been the most satisfying, the most stimulating and the most rewarding, not necessarily in financial terms, but in terms of sheer enjoyment. It offers the writer a lot of creative involvement, as the writer works very closely with the director, much more so than with television or radio. You attend rehearsals, make suggestions, re-write when necessary and are generally involved at every stage. Then comes the thrill of the opening night, the party afterwards, the wait to read what the critics have to say, followed by next morning's inquest on stage in the theatre; decisions are made as to how much needs cutting, whether the end of Act One needs a better line or would Act Two be improved with a quick rewrite . . . but we are getting ahead of ourselves. Sorry about that, but we do get carried away thinking about it all.

Writing for the theatre involves a certain technique not required in other forms of writing. The first thing you must always be aware of is the limitation of the theatre itself. You will have to think of an idea that can be developed into a play lasting two hours or so, yet which takes place, preferably, in one set. That's part of the attraction of writing for the theatre – it's a challenge. Of course it *is* possible, by using certain mechanics like a revolving stage or sliding scenery to create more than one set, but not all theatres are equipped to do this and most managements prefer plays that only require one set. An imaginative stage designer can, of course, work wonders with lighting, drapes, props and clever scenery, so there is still a lot which can be suggested within the confines of the basic set. The other challenge is to create a play which can be performed by only six or eight thespians (isn't that a lovely word? totally sexless). It's not impossible. Look at Willy Russell's award winning play *Shirley Valentine*. One set and a cast of one. We bet the theatre managements loved him for that! There are, of course, plays with quite large casts, but a play from a new writer will be looked at more favourably if it has a small cast and a single set.

Let us make it perfectly clear before we go any further that we are talking here about a stage play, either a drama or comedy, and not about a musical play. Musicals have a set of rules all of their own, and as one of us can't read a note of music, and the other is tone deaf, we wouldn't presume to try and tell you how to write a musical.

The best advice we can give you if you're thinking of an idea for a stage play, is to go to see as many plays as you can, both dramas and comedies. Study the sets and see how each writer uses the whole of the stage to keep the action going. Make a note of how many entrances and exits the set contains. Entrances and exits are very important – they can provide you with lots of opportunities to move the cast about, and almost take the place of another set. Notice how some sets have a set within a set – an alcove or a practical cloakroom – which again helps with the action.

The one big advantage a writer has with a stage play is that it is being performed live in front of an audience. The audience are watching real live flesh and blood actors and actresses, and not a recorded television or cinema performance. That fact alone holds their interest, so your play has a head start before the curtain rises. All you have to do is make sure that you don't lose that interest; make your characters sparkle, make the situations dramatic and gripping, or comic and witty, whichever the case may be. And, most important – never leave a character on stage for any length of time with nothing to say or nothing to do. Remember, the theatre audience can see the entire stage and everyone on it. A character just standing or sitting with nothing to say or do becomes a distraction. It disturbs the audience and embarrasses the actor or actress. If you can't invent some dialogue or action at that moment, find an excuse for the character to exit. Not only will that keep the audience's attention from wandering, it will give you another piece of action.

Now a word about the beginning of a play. When that curtain rises for the first time, what does the audience see? Well, they see the set. So if your story takes place in a drawing room, make it as interesting as you can. Think about it carefully. Does it have a french window? Very useful, that, for people to come in and go out by, or even hide behind if there are curtains. Is there a cocktail cabinet – always good for a bit of business. Is there a settee? And if there is does it convert to a put-u-up? In the right story, this could be a great help. Suppose some guests have arrived unexpectedly, or a couple's car has broken down and they beg shelter. The only available place for them to sleep may be the put-u-up. You can now play a 'bedroom' scene in the drawing room. So when you start to develop an idea it's vital to decide first what kind of set you need and to make the set work in your favour. After they've seen the set, the audience see who is occupying it. We have learned from past experience that if the curtain rises on a crowded stage the audience is confused. There is too much to take in at one time. The less people onstage the better. We would never recommend a curtain rising on more than two people onstage. Indeed we would go further. The best opening of a play is an empty stage. Let the audience see the set and take in the various bits of furniture. Then let the tension build for a few seconds before your first character makes an entrance. Every actor and actress needs to make an entrance. It's their way of saying 'I'm here, look at me.' It also helps the audience to meet each character separately, and to learn a little about them. It is useful in the writing inasmuch as you can use your characters to introduce others. For example, supposing the curtain rises on an empty drawing room:

(A FIGURE APPEARS AT THE FRENCH WINDOWS. IT IS HENRY BAXTER, A YOUNG MAN IN HIS EARLY TWENTIES. HE IS WEARING A BLAZER AND FLANNELS. HE PRESSES HIS FACE AGAINST THE WINDOW PANE AND RATTLES THE DOOR. HE RAPS ON THE GLASS AND MOUTHS 'HELLO'. WE CAN'T HEAR HIM.)

MARTHA   (OFFSTAGE. IN A QUAVERY VOICE) Just a minute. I'm coming.

(HENRY PRESSES HIS FACE AGAINST THE GLASS AGAIN, SHRUGS AND MOVES OUT OF SIGHT LEFT. MARTHA ENTERS. AN ELDERLY WOMAN. SHE SHUFFLES SLOWLY ACROSS THE ROOM TO THE WINDOW.)

MARTHA   Hello – where are you?

(SHE UNLOCKS THE WINDOW AND PEERS OUT.)

MARTHA   Are you there?

(SHE EXITS AND DISAPPEARS OUT OF SIGHT RIGHT. A PAUSE, THEN HENRY RETURNS. HE GOES TO RATTLE THE WINDOW, FINDS IT OPENS, AND ENTERS, CLOSING THE WINDOW BEHIND HIM.)

HENRY   (CALLING) Aunt Martha.

(BEHIND HIM, MARTHA APPEARS AT THE WINDOW AND KNOCKS. HENRY OPENS IT TO LET HER IN.)

HENRY   There you are Aunt.

MARTHA   There was somebody knocking at the window.

HENRY   It was me.

MARTHA   No it wasn't you dear. You're in here.

HENRY   (TRYING TO EXPLAIN) No what I mean is . . . (GIVING UP) Oh never mind. Has Uncle Albert arrived yet?

MARTHA   Not yet.

HENRY   Late as usual. He's so predictable. When he arrives he'll say the same old things he says every year. (MIMICKING) Here I am. Better late than never. My word, it doesn't seem a year since we last met. It's true what they say. *Tempus fugit.*

(ARTHUR POTTER ENTERS FROM THE HALL. A MIDDLE-AGED MAN, DRESSED IN TWEEDS.)

ARTHUR   Here I am. Better late than never. My word, it doesn't seen a year since we last met. It's true what they say. Time flies.

You see how the inclusion of the french windows can provide a little bit of comic action at the outset. And how Henry set up the entrance of Arthur. Arthur's repetition of Henry's mimicry is funny, and the fact that he changes his usual 'tempus fugit' to 'time flies' even funnier. This is the sort of thinking you should do to get the play off to a good start. A stage play can have two or three acts, and each act should end at some dramatic point in the play, designed to keep the audience eager to know what happens next. In between each act is a fifteen to twenty minute interval.

You may, if you wish to indicate the passage of time during an act, split the act so that in between scenes the curtain is lowered briefly to allow for a lighting or costume change. The last act must build towards a satisfactory climax, as it is this act which makes the most impression on an audience. If the rest of your play is brilliant and the last act poor, the audience will be left with the impression that the whole play was poor. They will, however, forgive a poor beginning if your last act is great. Of course what you should always aim for is to make your play good at the beginning, great in the middle and absolutely fabulous at the end.

Summing up

Just to remind you, let's list some of the important points to remember:
1 Films are above all a visual medium.
2 Think BIG.
3 Think international.
4 See as many films as you can.
5 A stage play is a challenge.
6 Aim for one set and six to eight characters.
7 Be inventive.
8 Go to the theatre as often as possible.

8. Writing for Pleasure

To the hardened professional writer, we are told, anyone who writes, but who doesn't write for money is an idiot. So it seems to us that the world is full of idiots.

The growth of creative writing classes bears witness to the increasing numbers of people who only write because they enjoy it. They form writing circles, where they chat over their ideas with friends and each meeting becomes a pleasurable social occasion, the high spot of the week, and a wonderfully therapeutic, relaxing form of self-expression.

Writing ambitions vary. Some people want to write short stories, others poems. Here and there you find someone who has a novel in mind. Some are concerned about many present-day problems and issues and write articles about them, but the fact remains that many people don't write with the intention of getting published. All they want to do is write; they can put their thoughts on paper without any outside pressures, and get enormous pleasure from doing so. It helps them to get rid of many of their nagging inhibitions and express what they really think. It gives them happiness. And that's important!

This applies to many students in creative writing classes where a lot of members come purely from pleasure, particularly to the evening classes. At work all day they crave relaxation in the evenings, and listening to other opinions, writing exercises they've been given and talking about their own ideas and problems seems to give them that.

Writing is for everyone who wants to write – there are no obstacles in your way. You don't need any qualifications, for a start, and your age doesn't bother anyone. Neither does your religion, race or colour.

As far as age is concerned, one of George's classes ranged from seventeen to eighty, and the eighty year old was just as bright and intelligent as anyone else in the class – perhaps even more so. In fact, everyone respected his wide knowledge and experience and he made many friends.

No! Writing for pleasure is on the increase and giving people a new interest in life. Why don't *you* give it a whirl?

Keeping a diary

You don't have to write a short story, or attempt what seems to be the mammoth task of writing a novel. There are loads of things to write about. What about keeping a diary, for instance?

We don't mean simply putting appointments down. Many people do that. We mean *writing* it! Put your appointments down by all means, but embellish them. Reveal your feelings in your diary.

Take an entry like this. 'Monday: the launderette.' Boring, isn't it – but was the visit to the launderette straighforward? Did you meet anyone on the way there or back? Did anything happen in the launderette? The simple entry of 'Monday: the launderette' could bring back many a grin or a grimace in a few years' time when you read it. Like this, perhaps . . .

Monday: What a bore – the launderette!
That's your initial entry. This is what could happen when you write it up on your return
I was wrong! How I was wrong! All started in the usual humdrum way. I was captured by old Mrs Willis talking about her cats and her son-in-law. It's the same thing every week, and I was resigned to it. Then we heard the blast of police whistles and two Panda Cars with their sirens going pulled up outside the bank opposite. Other Pandas blocked the exits and entrances to the street, and there were police all over the place. Then the shooting started. We all rushed to the window to look out, but the police ordered us back again. Old Mrs Willis stopped talking about her cats but nearly had kittens with the excitement. I wouldn't have missed it for worlds. Anyway, it was all over in ten minutes. Nobody could get in or out of the street, we all thought, but the robbers did. They got away with £75 000.

Do you see what we mean? It's not contrived. High street banks *are* burgled and *some*one's there to see it happen. It might be you!

But that's only one type of incident. If you take an interest in things around you, you'll find there are many entries for your diary just waiting for you to write about them. You'll see acts of kindness. You might meet someone you last saw twenty years ago. How did you feel about this? Fill in all the missing details and make your diary live. It's fun. What happened on your little daughter's birthday? It might well be worth recording. Refer to current events as well. After all, a diary isn't just a cold, day-to-day record of events; it is about *your* life. It'll all make absorbing reading, both for you and your family in years to come. Try it.

Personal reminiscences

Writing your personal reminiscences can be fun. Unlike a diary, which deals with each day as it happens, personal reminiscences deal with memories, perhaps combined with a touch of family history. Yet again, fascinating reading in the future, and a great source of pleasure for you.

Imagine how interesting you would find it if you came across some personal stories about your parents, grandparents and great-grandparents, and, moreover, written by them. Suddenly you're reading about a very personal past from a very personal viewpoint. A sheer joy, we would think. Something to treasure. You might read about how they faced up to their problems, just as you are trying to do; meeting the ever-present mortgage payments; trying to eke out the weekly money, and then, when times got a little easier, what they did for a 'treat'. Wonderful reading!

People always like writing about themselves. We all think that some parts of our lives would interest others, and this usually dawns on us in later years when we have 'lived a little'.

Again, on more than one occasion in creative writing classes, men or women in their sixties have admitted, almost shyly 'I'm starting on a novel – and there's more than a little of me in it . . .'

Well, you can call it an autobiography if you like, or you might say it's a collection of personal reminiscences, but whatever it is, the writer will have an enormously interesting time uncovering all those memories which make up a life.

Poetry

Poetry, alas, seems to be one of those art forms which is more popular with the writer than the reader. Perhaps more people write poetry for pleasure than anything else. But, so we are told, poetry is not easily sold.

Getting your poetry into print is terribly difficult, no matter how good you are. Peter Finch, the poet and publisher, has said that the average first print-run of a poetry book is a maximum of three hundred copies, so that gives you an idea of actual poetry sales and the limited chances you have of getting your work published.

Nevertheless, as we have just said, if people don't want to buy it they certainly want to write it, and there are many attractive poetry competitions springing up all the time to reward aspiring poets for their efforts.

'How do we start?' ask many would-be poets. With poetry, the advice is 'select your image, think about it and then write about it.' There is no better way to begin than by putting your thoughts on paper.

You might have a visual image you want to describe – a lake, or a river – or a feeling or emotion, so put your thoughts down. Don't worry if your subject has been written about by someone else. It's always a case of 'it's not what you do, it's the way that you do it'. William Wordsworth probably felt that he had said it all about daffodils when he 'wandered lonely as a cloud', but since then, the world has been inundated with poems about daffodils. 'Love' is another subject that will always make the world go round. Poets will write about it until the end of time.

Just remember that everyone sees things differently, and that everyone expresses their emotions in a different manner. You, too, will see your images differently from others and put your own personal stamp on your work.

You may choose to write poetry which rhymes, or you may prefer to work with unrhymed verse, often called 'free verse'. Again, this is entirely up to you, but whichever you choose, a thing to avoid is padding. If you find that your sentence is too short, don't add a word to make the metre conform, especially if the word you add doesn't help your line poetically. There is nothing more tempting then to put a 'do' or a 'just' into a line to make it scan correctly. For instance if you're going to write 'The Christmas tree glows' don't make it 'The Christmas tree *does* glow'. Apart from its being padding, it *looks* like padding. The less your rhyming looks deliberate and predictable, the better.

Above all, read the better poets and study them. Robin Skelton is a poet we particularly admire; he has written a very good introduction to poetry and how it works, listed in the 'recommended reading' list on p. 121.

It's impossible to be dogmatic about writing. Take the question of writer's block for instance. You reach the point where every imaginative thought dries up. You can't think of anything to write about, and you're firmly convinced that you'll never write a poem again. It's something which happens to all writers, so how do you get out of it? Well, different people have different ways, but in the end it's up to you, depending on your own personality and your way of working.

Some say it's better to wait for inspiration to strike. Otherwise if you force everything you could end up with a poem that looks stilted and 'cardboard', as if it was written in desperation.

Others say that by putting associative words on paper the creative juices will start to flow; this will enable you to discover your 'image' reasonably quickly and help you to get started.

Whatever suits you may not suit someone else – but if it's good for you, stay with it.

Letter writing

Letter writing is all too easily dismissed as a way of writing for pleasure. In fact, many people regard it as a chore. And it shouldn't be, if you approach it in the right frame of mind.

Just like keeping a diary, you should take a pride and interest in your letter and make it come alive. Write it to interest and amuse the reader. In other words, make it descriptive – even write it in the same way as you would a short story. And you would be surprised at the number of people who started off writing 'funny' letters and ended up as short story writers. Letters, funny or dramatic, seem to be a good starting point for the would-be writer.

We have conferred on this matter and found that we each used to take our letter writing seriously, thinking of it as a challenge. We used to look forward to it, happily anticipating the letter to come, working out how to make it read to its best advantage. We would each prepare lines and descriptions in advance, which gave us tremendous enjoyment even *before* we wrote the letter.

Even though we couldn't be there when the letter was opened and read, we looked forward to the reactions of the reader, and hoped that he or she would laugh when they read it. To us, writing a letter was like writing a comedy script for an audience. We put everything we had into it and had incredible fun in doing so. Neither of us will forget the hilarious times we had writing those letters for pleasure.

You should try it. Dramatic or funny, it's a fabulous pastime, and if you don't have a go you're missing something.

Get writing – and you'll enjoy it!

9. Useful Information

Presentation of manuscripts

The presentation of your work is particularly important, for it can mean the difference between your work being read or passed over. There is a standard procedure laid down, and it is in your interest to adhere to it.

Short stories and articles
White A4 paper should be used.

The first sheet is your 'cover sheet'. On this sheet, roughly half-way down, you type the title of your story or article in capitals and underline it.

Beneath it, say a double space below, state the approximate number of words in the piece. A couple of inches below this, type your name in lower case and underline it, and then, towards the left-hand corner of the page type your name and address.

If you have written an article and are enclosing photographs to illustrate your points, type in the number of enclosures along with the approximate wordage.

On sheet 1 of your story or article, about a third of the way down, type the title in capital letters in the middle, and about 1–1½ inches beneath this, type your name in lower case and underline it.

A clear margin should be left on either side of the page, roughly 1½–2 inches on the left side, and 1 inch or so on the right. Type the text double spaced.

On the following pages you should also leave a margin of 1 inch or so at the top and the bottom of each page.

Sometimes pages become separated from each other, and so it is usual – and a worthwhile precaution – to put a key word from your title at the top of each page, together with your surname. For instance, if your title is *Anyone For Tennis?* and your name is Nancy

Bloggs, you might use the word 'tennis' as your key word, together with your surname Bloggs. At the top of each page in this case, you would type Tennis/Bloggs, and follow it with the page number.

In all cases, it is advised that you should enclose a stamped addressed envelope.

The covering letter to the editor should be short and business-like, but if you have any special qualifications relating to your article's subject it is just as well to mention them.

It is worth finding out the editor's name, so that when you write your letter you can address it personally – this will be appreciated.

Novels
The presentation of a novel is much the same as for short stories and articles. Type on A4 paper, double spaced.

A stamped addressed envelope is again recommended with your manuscript, but don't send the entire novel. Most publishers would prefer to see a synopsis and a couple of chapters to start off with.

Radio comedy
Radio comedy presentation, bless it, hasn't changed much through the years, except when sound effects are wanted; whereas writers used to type F/X: they now sometimes type TAPE:. This is because sound effects are now all on tape.

About ½ inch in from the left-hand side of your sheet of A4, type the name of the speaker in caps. If at that point you want TAPE or F/X. type them in instead, also in caps. The same goes for GRAMS (meaning 'music'). Use double spacing.

Number the speeches (including the lines where you have typed TAPE and GRAMS) consecutively down the page until you come to the bottom. Then begin again on the next page, and so on.

About 2½ inches in from the side of the page, your dialogue, or grams or effects should be typed, the dialogue in lower case, and the effects and music in caps. The effects and music should be underlined from the side of the page, where you have signified you want them (see page 58). Where music is needed substitute GRAMS for TAPE or APPLAUSE. A cover sheet is necessary.

Radio drama
Half an inch from the left-hand side of your sheet of paper you type your scene number. Under the scene number you type in

caps, EXTERIOR or INTERIOR, depending on where your scene takes place, followed by NIGHT or DAY, depending on when it takes place.

As in radio comedy, you type in your characters' names here, numbering each speech consecutively until the bottom of the page, starting again with '1' on the next page. The names should be in caps.

The dialogue lines start approximately 2½ inches in, in lower case; directions should be about 3 inches in, enclosed in brackets, underlined and typed in caps.

Opposite the scene number, also in brackets, caps and under-lined, are your scene and sound descriptions. For drama, how-ever, you should not type F/X. or TAPE. Just describe simply what is happening. For example:

SCENE 1:   (A SHIP AT SEA. A HURRICANE IS BLOWING. IT IS
EXTERIOR. DAY.   RAINING HEAVILY.)
1. DIALOGUE: Starts here.
           (THE SOUND OF A SAIL TEARING, THE CREAK OF
           BREAKING WOOD AND SOMETHING HEAVY
           CRASHING DOWN ON DECK.)

Although it sometimes varies, single spacing is generally used for the description and double for the dialogue, with an extra single spacing dividing the speeches.

You will need a cover sheet as described above, but you don't need to include a word count.

Television

Leave a margin of about 4 inches on the left-hand side of the sheet. Your directions and descriptions should be in capitals, and dia-logue should be double-spaced with an extra single-spacing in between speeches. Character names should be in caps and placed directly above the dialogue, then underlined. Don't worry about camera angles, they're not your problem, unless you have a par-ticular shot in mind.

Set the scene, like this:

1. INT. GEORGE'S GARAGE. DAY.

A title or cover sheet should be typed, as you would for a short story, but you don't need to state number of words written. Dia-logue is in lower case.

Films

Again you need a cover sheet as described above, without the word count. Most companies would prefer to see the full screen play.

In the case of screenplays for films, the description of the action, etc. is in lower case, not caps. The names are in caps.

Space your dialogue out, and double space the directions from the dialogue, but put the stage directions themselves in single spacing.

Unless you wish to make a point, don't give too many camera directions.

Each scene should be numbered on the left as in television, with EXTERIOR or INTERIOR as the case may be, the setting of the scene, and whether it is NIGHT or DAY.

Leave a margin of about 1½ inches on the left, and a reasonable margin on the right-hand side.

A sample screenplay should look something like this:

3. EXT. HOUSE. DAY.

JO goes across to the car, then turns and throws the keys to GEORGE.

JO
Here, you drive.
(In this case, we have put the name above the speech, but it can also be placed at the side. Presentations vary.)

The stage

Leave a ½ inch margin on the left, type the character's name in caps. Two inches in from the name, the dialogue should be typed in lower case.

Approximately 1 inch in from the beginning of the dialogue you type your instructions in lower case.

All names, even in the descriptions, should be in caps. There should be single spacing between the lines of dialogue and description; double spacing between speeches, and between the speeches and description.

For example:
GEOFF   Why didn't you take a taxi?
VINCE   You can never find one in the rain.
            GEOFF offers him a whisky.
            VINCE shakes his head.

VINCE   (sits down) I'm off it. Got a beer?

Again, you will need a cover sheet, with the title about a third of the way down. About half the way down, you put a description of your play, such as:

DEAD BODIES

A COMEDY THRILLER

by Adrian Smithers

Agent's name   *Your name*
Address   *Address*

Agents

Agents are generally not interested in taking on new writers, especially in the short story category. In any case, most short story editors have their own rates of payment and you have to take it or leave it.

New writers will find it very hard work to find an agent who will get them work, let alone sell work you have already written, but should you sell something worthwhile, such as a book, film or television or radio script, most agents will negotiate your contract for you. Having done this, and knowing the quality of your work, it is likely that they will act for you from then on, but in the initial stages it is up to you to do it yourself.

For details of agents, both literary and those specialising in plays, films, television and radio, the *Writers' and Artists' Yearbook* is a fount of information, telling you virtually all you want to know about them.

Where to send your scripts

Radio

Writing for the BBC by Norman Longmate (BBC Books) gives complete and comprehensive coverage of all BBC Radio's requirements; it also lists addresses, including all local radio stations. For scripts to be sent to BBC Headquarters, however, you should put the name of the department to which your script is to be delivered – Drama, Light Entertainment, etc – and address it to:

Broadcasting House
Portland Place
London W1A 1AA

The BBC will do the rest.

As far as independent or BBC local radio is concerned, to our knowledge, no regular slots for drama and short stories exist. However, they encourage talks, and occasionally their policy changes to allow excursions into drama and light entertainment. It is well worth keeping in touch with your local radio station and keeping up-to-date with their requirements.

Again, the invaluable *Writers' and Artists' Yearbook* comes into its own here, with the names and addresses of all the local and independent radio stations you could want.

Television

BBC TELEVISION The BBC has two TV channels to itself. Put the name of the script department for which your script is intended – Drama or Light Entertainment – and send it to:

BBC Television
Television Centre
Wood Lane, Shepherds Bush
London W12 7RJ

INDEPENDENT PRODUCTIONS Small, independent production companies are springing up continually these days. The BBC alone allots 25 per cent of its output to private companies, who make the programmes and then sell to the BBC.

For details of these companies, we would recommend you to the Independent Programme Producers Association (IPPA) *Members' Directory* (Kays Publishing Company).

COMMERCIAL TELEVISION Again, address your script to the relevant department. A list of stations follows:

Anglia Television Ltd, Anglia House, Norwich NR1 3JG

Border Television Ltd, Television Centre, Carlisle CA1 3NT

Central Television PLC, Central House, Broad Street, Birmingham B1 2JP

Channel Four Ltd, 56–62 Charlotte Street, London W1P 2AX

Grampian Television Ltd, Queens Cross, Aberdeen AB9 2XL

Granada Television Ltd, Television Centre, Manchester M60 9EA

HTV Ltd, Television Centre, Bath Road, Brislington, Bristol BS4 3HG

London Weekend Television Ltd, South Bank Television Centre, Kent House, Upper Ground, London SE1 9LT

Scottish Television Ltd, Cowcaddens, Glasgow G2 3PR

Television South West Ltd, Derrys Cross, Plymouth PL1 2SP

Television South PLC, Television Centre, Northam, Southampton SO9 4YQ

Thames Television Ltd, Teddington Studios, Broom Road, Teddington, Middlesex TW11 9NT

Tyne Tees Television Ltd, Television Centre, City Road, Newcastle-Upon-Tyne NE1 2AL

Ulster Television Ltd, Havelock House, Ormeau Road, Belfast BT7 1EB

Yorkshire Television Ltd, Television Centre, Leeds LS3 1JS

Theatre

It is difficult for a new or unknown writer to find a market for his play with professional managements, and one possible solution is to find an amateur dramatic group who would be willing to present it.

Should you undertake the daunting task of writing a play, we would again suggest you buy or borrow a copy of *Writers' and Artists' Year Book*. The book really is a boon for all writers, and the section in it under the heading of 'Markets for Stage Plays' will tell you all you need to know. Not only does it give you a comprehensive list of markets for your play, both London and provincial, but it tells you about the publishers who specialise in the publication of plays, the financial help given by the Arts Council of Great Britain and various other awards.

Films

Much of the market for screenplays these days is concerned with the making of films for television. *Writers' and Artists' Yearbook* offers advice and gives a list of markets for those interested.

Payment

Payment varies enormously and changes from year to year, so it is well-nigh impossible to give amounts. However, here is a summing up of how the various markets approach payment for accepted work.

Short stories
The fee is swayed by the price and readership of the magazine. The magazine *Bella* pays at present £150 for a story of 1500 words, and less for shorter stories. The more expensive and glossy the magazine, the more they will pay, but the harder it is for you to get your work accepted.

In general, they each have their payments worked out. Some pay depending on the number of words and some pay a flat fee.

Non-fiction
Again, it depends on the quality and readership of the magazine or newspaper, some of which pay on the number of words and some a flat fee. In some cases, £80.00 for an article of a thousand words is considered good for a beginner. On the whole, local papers pay less.

Radio
BBC Radio has its own rates of pay, working upwards from the beginner to the established writer. The Writers' Guild of Great Britain has negotiated a minimum fee for all types of writing, and this applies to all writers. Unless you can offer a very good reason for a suggested increase, they seldom budge from the rates laid down.

Independent Radio's rates are usually below those of the BBC, but both are negotiable.

Television
The Writers' Guild of Great Britain has agreed minimum fees with all companies, but the fees are negotiable.

Films & stage
As above.

Summing up
The *Writers' and Artists' Yearbook* gives a certain amount of advice

on how different markets pay. We are told that in all cases, should you wish to know the rates of payment for a particular piece of work, the best thing to do is to ring up the Editorial Department of magazines and newspapers for journalism and short stories, and to contact the Copyright Department for television and radio.

The Writers' Guild of Great Britain and the Society of Authors give advice on rates of pay and royalties to their members who are book writers. Rates of pay vary from publisher to publisher and have to be negotiated individually.

Recommended Reading

We would recommend the following books to anyone who is considering writing creatively, whether intending to start a writing career, or writing for pleasure. They are full of useful information and make worthwhile reading.

Television
How To Write Comedy by Brad Ashton (Elm Tree Books)
Writing for Television by Malcolm Hulke (A & C Black)
The Way to Write For Television by Eric Paice (Elm Tree Books)

Radio
The Way To Write Radio Drama by William Ash (Elm Tree Books)

Novels
Plotting And Writing Suspense Fiction by Patricia Highsmith (Popular Press). Includes both novels and short stories.
The Craft of Novel Writing by Dianne Doubtfire (Allison & Busby)
Writing The Novel by Lawrence Block (Writer's Digest)
Writing A Novel by John Braine (Methuen)

Basics and research
Writers' Questions Answered by Gordon Wells (Allison & Busby)
Writing for Pleasure and Profit by Michael Leggat (Hale)
The Nuts and Bolts of Writing by Michael Leggat (Hale)

Poetry
How To Publish Your Poetry by Peter Finch (Allison & Busby)
The Way To Write Poetry by Michael Baldwin (Elm Tree Books)
The Practice of Poetry by Robin Skelton (Heinemann)

Manuals

Roget's Thesaurus Of English Words And Phrases (Penguin)
The Concise Oxford Dictionary (Oxford University Press)
The Oxford Dictionary of Quotations (Oxford University Press)
Writers' & Artists' Yearbook (A & C Black)
As we have already mentioned in this chapter, this book is a mine of information and is a 'must' for all writers.
The Writer's Handbook (Macmillan)
The Poet's Manual and Rhyming Dictionary by Frances Stillman (Thames & Hudson)
The Concise Oxford Dictionary of Proverbs edited by J. A. Simpson (Oxford University Press)

Index